TURNING POINT

Judaism, Christianity and Islam Confront Greek Philosophy

A Dialogue with Holy Roman Emperor Frederick II

Jeff Bergner

Rambling Ridge Press, LLC
416 Wilderness Drive
Locust Grove, Virginia 22058

Bergner, Jeffrey T.
Turning Point: Judaism, Christianity and Islam Confront Greek Philosophy

Jeff Bergner.

LCCN 2021947607
ISBN 978-0-9890402-4-2 Hardcover
ISBN 978-0-9890402-5-9 Softcover

1. Judaism 2. Christianity 3. Islam 4. Greek Philosophy 5. HRE Frederick II

Printed in the United States of America.

manifestare ea quae sunt, sicut sunt
(to set forth the things which are, as they are)

Frederick II

Introduction

On February 18, 1248 Holy Roman Emperor Frederick II went hunting with his beloved falcons. At that time he and his forces were camped outside the city of Parma, laying siege to the city. After the all but certain surrender of Parma, Frederick intended to raze Parma and replace it with a new city named Victoria, which Frederick was already beginning to construct on the site of his encampment.

Frederick expected no offensive action from Parma that day, and felt safe to take his best troops to hunt with him. In his absence, however, Parma surprised and completely overran Frederick's camp.

It is well known that Frederick lost much of value that day. He lost valuable jewels, substantial sums of money and his entire traveling library. Among the books known to have been lost that day was Frederick's own manuscript *De Arte Venandi cum Avibus* (*The Art of Hunting with Birds*).

※ ❊ ❊ ❊ ※

In the Prologue to *de Arte* Frederick described himself not simply as a falconer or even as the Holy Roman Emperor, but as a "lover of wisdom with a philosophic and speculative mind." The present volume is a dialogue I have created which reflects just this. Throughout his life Frederick sought out and conversed regularly with the leading scholars of ancient Greek philosophy and the three monotheistic faiths of his—and of our own—day. This dialogue displays the fruit of those conversations.

We live today at a time in which the balance between religious faith and Enlightenment reason has tipped very far in favor of the latter. As a result, we do not often experience today the depth of thinking which occurred when religious doctrines were being seriously challenged in the west for the first time in nearly a thousand years. The ongoing debate between faith and reason—which is unlikely ever to be fully settled—received its deepest formulation in the years in which Greek philosophy, and particularly Aristotle, were re-discovered in the west.

The late twelfth and early thirteenth centuries were a turning point in the thought of the west. This was the age of Averroes, Maimonides and Aquinas, each of whom struggled to find the proper balance between their respective faiths of Islam, Judaism and Christianity and ancient Greek pagan philosophy. Moreover, this was the age when each faith discovered that the others were engaged in the very same process. Much intellectual borrowing took place, especially from Arab thought to Judaism and Christianity.

Both today's advocates of the monotheistic faiths and the advocates of secular reason will find much to be learned from this period. The many issues debated then will be familiar today, though likely not at the same level and depth. As John Stuart Mill famously said, "He who knows only his own side of the case knows little of that. He must be able to know [the opinions of his adversary] from persons who actually believe them … He must know them in their most plausible and persuasive form."

Is the world eternal or created? Can something be created from nothing? Why does the world exist just as it does, and not otherwise? Does God's existence have a purpose? Are all descriptions of God simply qualities which humans admire? Does God necessarily act from reason? Can God's omnipotence and human free will be reconciled? Can there be a proper name for God? Does God exist in a place, or everywhere and nowhere? Do heaven and hell exist in a place? Can we learn ethics from reason alone? These are among the questions which this dialogue addresses.

Why Frederick II? Frederick was not only the beneficiary of the re-discovery of Aristotle but also its champion. He commissioned translations of many Greek and Arab works into Latin and Hebrew. He is said to have spoken five or six languages himself, including Arabic which he learned as a youth in Sicily. As Holy Roman Emperor he was in a position to facilitate conversations and written exchanges with a broad range of philosophers and religious scholars. He knew indirectly, and often directly, all the leading intellectual and political figures of his day. He was of course more than familiar with the six popes who reigned during his lifetime, having now better and now worse relationships with them. Throughout all the ups and downs, however, he remained a staunch and consistent defender of the secular rights of the Emperor. He was excommunicated on three separate occasions.

Frederick brought to his court both Michael Scot, the foremost astrologer of the age, and Jacob Anatoli, the Jewish scholar of the ibn Tibbon family which favored the works of Maimonides. Both translated works of Aristotle and Averroes' commentaries on Aristotle into Latin and Hebrew. Both Bishop Albert (later to be known as Albertus Magnus) and the young Thomas of Aquino were known personally to Frederick, as both their fathers were employed in Frederick's service.

Frederick was also acquainted with Francis of Assisi, with whom he shared somewhat the same hope of a church which was purer, simpler and poorer than the papacy in Rome had become. On one occasion Francis traveled to Egypt to meet with the Muslim leader al-Kamil, the nephew of the great Arab conqueror Saladin. Some years later Frederick himself led a crusade to the Middle East to regain Christian control of Jerusalem which had been cut off since Saladin's victory in 1187. He negotiated directly with the same al-Kamil, with whom he maintained a respectful relationship. In doing so he achieved a ten year truce to re-open Jerusalem to Christians, the only crusade to do so without shedding massive amounts of blood.

Frederick sponsored and took part in the creation of a new kind of poetry based for the first time on colloquial Italian, a form which Dante later perfected. In doing this Frederick was aided by his courtier Piero della Vigna, who unfortunately later came to grief with Frederick over rumors of suspected treachery.

Frederick sought out Leonardo of Pisa, whom we know today as Fibonacci. Leonardo, the man who brought Arabic numerals to the west, was arguably the greatest mathematician of his day. Leonardo communicated with Frederick's court philosopher Master Theodore, and dedicated his famous *Liber Quadratorum* to Frederick.

Frederick also founded the first secular university in the west at Naples. His purpose in doing so, beyond general enlightenment, was to train legal scholars to serve his government in southern Italy and Sicily. This government, for which he published the legal code of the *Liber Augustalis* in 1232, was the most rationalized, law-based government of the age and is a precursor of the modern administrative state. Frederick favored freedom of thought and expression and opposed efforts to suppress these freedoms, such as when works of Aristotle, Averroes and others were burned in Paris in 1210. Though he made exceptions on several occasions, Frederick is known to have fostered toleration of differing faiths to a degree unknown at the time.

In short, there was scarcely an intellectual figure of any consequence, or a subject of any importance which was unknown to Frederick and in which he did not play a leading role. It was not without reason he was called during his lifetime *stupor mundi* (wonder of the world).

The dialogue is titled *The Book of the Sun,* for reasons the text makes clear. It is set in the 1240's, as a conversation between Frederick and his court philosopher Master Theodore, who succeeded Michael Scot in that position. I have based Frederick's views as closely as possible to what is known of them, though I doubtless have extended and elaborated on them in many places. Quotations in the text consist of words spoken or written by Frederick which have come down to us in the historical record. I have made every effort to avoid anachronisms—reading back in time more modern thoughts and actions—though an alert reader might find two places where I took small liberties.

The dialogue reflects Frederick's firsthand familiarity with contemporary Jewish, Christian and Islamic thought. It also displays his familiarity with Plato's *Timaeus*, a portion of which was the only directly available Platonic dialogue at the time. And it features centrally Frederick's lifelong struggle with the church over the political and material preoccupations of the papacy of the time.

The dialogue expresses Frederick's rather low opinion of what was known of Plato's political thought from many secondary accounts. Frederick preferred Aristotle's political thought. Although Frederick commissioned translations of Aristotle and of Averroes' commentaries on Aristotle, he was not an uncritical admirer of Aristotle's works, especially those on nature. He corrected Aristotle wherever he thought it was necessary. One might say that ancient Rome was the greatest source of Frederick's political ideas.

At the same time, Frederick celebrates Plato's importance as a philosopher, including and especially Plato's thinking about what he called Ideas. Frederick favors Plato's Ideas, though his interpretation is admittedly through an Aristotelian lens. The dialogue makes clear Frederick's well-known fondness for the natural world as well as his methods of observation to achieve knowledge about it.

Frederick is not an entirely modern man, as his extended thoughts on government especially make clear. But one can find in him many hints of things to come, including the Protestant Reformation, early modern science and the idea of a tolerant secular administrative state.

Friedrich Nietzsche called Frederick "the *first* European to my taste" and one of only a small number of "delightfully and unimaginable people." For anyone who wishes to understand better the axial issues regarding faith and reason, relationships between the thinkers of the three monotheistic faiths, and the respective roles of religion and government, there are few better places to look.

Lake of the Woods, Virginia
October, 2021

CONTENTS

The Book of the Sun

Frederick II

Romanorum imperatore

Semper augustus;

Jerusalem et Siciliae Rex

PROLOGUE

Frederick II: You are familiar, I suppose, with the legend of the sleeping king who will return one day to bring glory and salvation to his people?

Master Theodore: Yes, your excellency. It is a story often told about your grandfather Frederick Barbarossa. It is said that he sleeps in a mountain cave and will return one day. I have heard it said about you too, that perhaps you will be the sleeping king who will return one day.

Frederick II: Yes, I have heard that too. What do you think, Master Theodore, are these stories true?

Master Theodore: As a philosopher, I am wary of predicting the future. Perhaps this is a question better suited to your court astrologer. But it seems there is nothing in the world which you and I study each day to suggest this is true. In truth, the notion seems rather far-fetched. What do you think?

Frederick II: I supposed you would say that. And I take no offense at it. But what if I told you the stories are true?

Master Theodore: I would be very surprised. But your words are opaque.

Frederick II: Let me explain. These stories will come true, but not in the way simple people imagine. A man who looks like me will not return. No, not that way at all.

Master Theodore: How so then?

Frederick II: What if I were to tell you that just now, even at this moment, you are playing a role in my return?

Master Theodore: I am still mystified.

Frederick II: Do you think the deeds of men can live on beyond them?

Master Theodore: Yes, of course. The founders of great empires leave their mark long after they die. Your deeds in shaping the empire you rule over will surely survive you. Is this what you mean?

Frederick II: My empire hopefully will survive and prosper. Much depends on my sons, especially Manfred. But I am saying something quite different. Are the deeds of men all that survive them? Is it not also the same with the works of the mind? Do we not have before us today the deep and penetrating words of the one who is rightly called The Philosopher? Haven't the words of Aristotle lived on for 1,500 years after his death? Are these words less important today than when they were written?

Master Theodore: Yes, that is true. Even the thoughtful adherents of today's three monotheistic faiths look to his words to help them know their faiths better.

Frederick II: Yes, it is true for Maimonides among the Jews, Averroes among the Muslims, and Peter Abelard, William of Auvergne, Robert Grosseteste and the great Albert among the Christians. Perhaps it will even be true one day of our young friend Thomas of Aquino.

Master Theodore: Yes, there are many examples.

Frederick II: Is this not also true of the founders of the three monotheistic faiths themselves—of Moses, Jesus and Muhammad? Here I may say something that will surprise you. You know firsthand how much blood and toil I have spent to unify my empire. You know how much effort I have expended to keep the popes within their proper bounds. This has been a heavy burden which I inherited from my ancestors and which I will leave to my sons.

Master Theodore: I know this struggle shapes each day for you.

Frederick II: It appears that the words of our deepest thinkers far outlive the deeds of our political rulers. Consider Aristotle himself. He was the tutor of Alexander, who created the largest empire the world had ever known. Alexander's empire is gone but Aristotle's words remain.

Or Moses. The government of Moses has long since passed away.

The Jews no longer rule over their former territory but are dispersed in many places. Yet the words of Moses live on.

Or Jesus. He governed no territory at all, nor even seemed to wish to. His words survive today and are looked to by many millions of people in both the east and west.

Or Muhammad. The empire of the Muslims has grown and shrunk and grown again. If the wily popes have their way and tempt future emperors into further crusades perhaps it will shrink again. Through all these fortunes the words of Muhammad are looked to today by the people of many lands.

Master Theodore: Yes, it does seem that the words of men can outlive men's deeds.

Frederick II: This is exactly what I wish to say to you: the thoughts and words of men often far outlive their deeds. I have struggled each day, even before I was crowned emperor to defend and expand my family's empire. But I do not suppose it will last forever. My thoughts—which I have explored with you and my friend, your esteemed predecessor Michael Scot—have a far greater chance to survive.

Master Theodore: I begin to see. But what words will you leave? Your book on the art of falconry is a masterpiece. It contains not only the best possible information on hunting birds, but is a model of careful observation in which you have corrected Aristotle in many places where he was mistaken. But this is surely not what you mean.

Frederick II: Of course not. You will help me write the words which will survive. You will write down our conversation. These will be the words which will return one day. These will be the words by which I will return and offer guidance not only to my former empire but to all people who are capable to understand them.

Master Theodore: I would of course be pleased to take part in this work. Your wide-ranging intellectual talents are well known in many lands. Your talents are such that you are called *stupor mundi* (the wonder of the world). But what distinctive views do you have? What message, comparable to those men of whom you have spoken, do you wish to leave? What will you teach?

Frederick II: We will come to that, Master Theodore. Let me begin by saying that we live in a very unusual time. For many centuries Christian theologians and philosophers have considered the relation of pagan philosophy to Christianity. Above all one might think of Augustine who found parallels between Platonism—more likely from Plotinus than Plato himself—and Christianity. There is nothing new in this. Before Augustine there was Origen and around his time there were the church fathers of Cappadocia. These thinkers interpreted pagan philosophy in terms of its consistency with Christian doctrine and judged these philosophies by how closely they comported with Christian doctrine. Where they aligned with Christian doctrine they were accepted. Augustine, for example, found much to admire in Platonism, which he charitably regarded as a secular precursor of Christianity. Where pagan philosophy did not comport with Christian doctrine, however, it was rejected.

Master Theodore: Is this not also true of the Jews?

Frederick II: Some very ancient Jews knew of Greek philosophy, and especially Plato. The historian Flavius Josephus even argues that Platonism was derived from earlier Hebrew doctrines. And Philo of Alexandria, who is not much known among the Jews today, aimed to Platonize scripture by finding everywhere within it allegories which were consistent with Platonic teaching. But during the last millennia the Jews have not been much influenced by pagan philosophy, tending rather to interpret and re-interpret their own scriptures. Maimonides rightly says that in many instances the Jews were prevented from access to pagan philosophy by those who tyrannized over them. At times one sees certain questions raised by pagan philosophers, but for the most part the Jews have maintained their own traditions largely unaffected by pagan philosophy until recent times.

Master Theodore: And the Muslims? Have they not also grappled with pagan philosophy?

Frederick II: Yes, in a way very parallel to Christian thinkers. Al-Kindi, al-Farabi, Avicenna and al-Ghazali, to name the most prominent, wrestled with how pagan philosophy could be consistent with Muhammad's teachings. Where they found support for Islamic doctrine in pagan philosophy they praised it; where they did not they rejected it. This tradition is also very old. It differs from the Christian west mainly in that it knew Aristotle far earlier and far better. Some, like Avicenna sought to reconcile a Platonized Aristotle with what they knew of Plato. But the Arabs knew far more of Aristotle's works than did we in the west.

Master Theodore: What then is different now?

Frederick II: Everything is different today. The three monotheistic faiths have become far better known to one another. We see in our lifetime a growing awareness of each other on the part of the three monotheistic faiths. We see each of these faiths discovering that it is not only its own faith, but each of the faiths that wrestle with their relationship to pagan philosophy. They are learning from one another.

Master Theodore: You have greatly encouraged this process yourself.

Frederick II: Yes, Master Theodore, I have sponsored many translations of thoughtful writers so that their works might be more widely available. I have particularly encouraged translations from Arabic to Latin and Hebrew, that these authors might be better understood in the west. Michael Scot has translated Aristotle's *On the Heavens* and *On the Soul* from Arabic, along with Averroes' commentaries. He has also translated Aristotle's zoological works into Latin. And our friend Jacob Anatoli, who I invited to come from France to Naples, has worked closely with Michael Scot. As you know, he is related to Samuel ibn Tibbon of the distinguished ibn Tibbon family of rabbis who are great admirers of Maimonides. Jacob Anatoli has translated Averroes' commentaries on Aristotle's logical and astronomical works, as well as Ptolemy's *Almagest*. There are many other examples as well.

Master Theodore: What has been the result of these efforts?

Frederick II: They are twofold. First, Aristotle's work has become far better known in the west. It is easy enough to equate Plato's demiurge in the *Timaeus* with the world-creating gods of the Jews, Christians and Muslims. With Aristotle this is more difficult, because he argues that the world has existed forever. Some have tried to equate Aristotle's first mover with a world-creating god, but this is not so easy. Aristotle's first mover is arrived at by logical necessity rather than speculations which Plato calls only "probable." And Aristotle's unmoved first mover is responsible only for the origin of motion, as opposed to the Jewish, Christian and Islamic gods whose creators are responsible for all being itself.

Master Theodore: I take your point. But is this all?

Frederick II: No. There is something far more important. Each tradition has long wrestled with the claims of philosophy and faith, the claims of reason and revelation. Each accords a role to reason but a far greater role to revelation. When reason can take us no further, there is revelation.

Master Theodore: As you say, this has been true for a long time. What is new?

Frederick II: What is new is this. So long as there is only one set of revelations, it is not so strange to think that revelation might take us beyond reason. As I will explain a bit later, what we know through our intellect is in a way also revealed to us. But now we see clearly three different sets of revelations. What shall we make of this? Would a god choose to illuminate some revelations to the Jews, different revelations to the Christians and still different revelations to the Muslims? What would be the point of that? The old question remains: what can we know by reason alone? But there is a new question: is there any reason to prefer one set of revelations to another, or to prefer any at all?

Master Theodore: If all these revelations were different, but still compatible with one another, this problem would not exist.

Frederick II: Yes, Master Theodore, just so. But they are not. Neither the Jews nor the Muslims believe that Jesus was a god. Neither the Jews nor the Christians believe that Muhammad received a divinely inspired message from an angel. And neither the Christians nor the Muslims believe the Torah of Moses is either necessary or sufficient for salvation. These are not small differences, but ones which go to the core of their faiths. There are portions of the three faiths which are compatible, but it would be foolish to think that their differences can be reconciled.

Master Theodore: Yes, it seems that a choice must be made as to what to take on faith.

Frederick II: Perhaps. It would be very strange for a god, especially one who is thought of as perfect, to illuminate men in ways that cannot be reconciled. Moreover, it seems there is no way in which men of one faith can hope to convert men of another faith by pointing to their own revelation. Indeed, it is difficult for men of one faith to speak coherently to men of another faith about their revelations.

Master Theodore: Is there a way forward?

Frederick II: Here is my point. What the three monotheistic faiths of our day can agree upon is what can be known about their god, or any god, by natural reason alone. The best thinkers of each faith seem to recognize this. This we see in the extraordinary thinkers that have emerged among all three faiths. No Muslim thinker has ever thought more deeply about how far reason can take us than Ibn Rushd, or Averroes as we in the west call him. He stands at the pinnacle of thought about how far reason can take us toward a true knowledge of god. And so too with Moses Maimonides. No Jewish thinker has surpassed his ability to consider the claims of Judaism on the basis of reason or philosophy. And among Christians we find many who have learned from Averroes and Maimonides and who are now open to a fair consideration of this question. This is surely so for Grosseteste in England, William of Auvergne in France and our own Albert in Germany. Each has achieved new heights of thought through their familiarity not only with those of their own tradition but with Averroes and Maimonides as well.

Master Theodore: Yes, it seems the traditions have influenced one another in very deep ways.

Frederick II: But it is more than this. Philosophy or natural reason is no longer useful only as a tool with which to defend the faiths. It has become something quite different. It has become the only basis upon which the most thoughtful advocates of each tradition can agree with one another. One of our Christian theologians has said that in reaching out to pagans and Muslims "Here we must have recourse to natural reason, to which all men are forced to assent." This is the point I wish to make, not only in regard to Muslims and pagans but in regard to all faiths: reason has a universal claim upon human beings which revelations do not.

Master Theodore: This overturns many hundreds of years of tradition.

Frederick II: Yes. It is not only that nothing in revelation can be inconsistent with reason, which is true. It is that the meaning and value of revelations themselves must be judged by reason. Reason takes us where it can in our knowledge of god. Where it cannot, faith in revelation steps in. But these revelations do not command universal assent.

Master Theodore: How then are we to choose among the competing revelations of Moses, Jesus and Muhammad?

Frederick II: This becomes a matter of reason itself. Averroes, for example, makes a long and detailed argument about why the faith of Islam is best. He does so by considering its utility, its practical effects on people, not its intrinsic revealed truth. And so too with Maimonides, who seeks to explain the superior virtue of the many laws which the Jews are to obey. And so too does Abelard, who argues the superiority of Christianity over Judaism because of its promise of not only temporal rewards but eternal rewards.

Master Theodore: These are very practical grounds upon which to prefer one revelation over another.

Frederick II: Yes, and as pragmatic grounds they are judged by— reason. Reason in this way is still a helper of revelation, but in a new way: as its judge.

Master Theodore: Shall we expect then that the religious traditions of faith will disappear in favor of human reason?

Frederick II: No, Master Theodore. This is not to be expected among the masses of people. The language of revelation speaks to humans who neither can nor even wish to employ their reason. They neither wish to know what can be known of god only by reason, nor upon what basis their revelations exist. This is why the most thoughtful advocates of reason—unless they reside in my kingdom— must be very careful. To contradict, or even to question the claims of their own traditions is to court grave danger. We should expect no end to religious traditions. Indeed, as I will explain these traditions have great use for the ends of government.

But for the most thoughtful men, whatever their own tradition, all is very different today. The entire foundations of thought are turned upside down. It may well be that god illuminates us, as the traditions say, but if he does so it is in teaching us how to think. To ask what we can know of god by reason alone, and then to judge the claims of revelation by these standards—this is to shake the foundation of the thought of our time.

Master Theodore: I believe I understand the depth of your claims. And it strikes me to say that they are likely to have many and far-reaching consequences.

Frederick II: Yes, Master Theodore. What I propose to do in our conversation is to consider all these matters. We will consider carefully the most thoughtful exponents of each faith to discover what truths they believe can be known about god by human reason alone. We will consider what this means for how we live and especially for what is the purpose of government. And we will consider the ways we can and cannot know about the world in which we live and how we should carry ourselves bravely within it.

ON JUDAISM

Frederick II: Let us consider first the teaching of the Jews, the oldest of the three monotheistic faiths.

Creation

And let us begin with the very first of these teachings, which concerns the creation of the world. This teaching is also accepted by Christians and Muslims. The wise Jews with whom I have spoken do not regard this account as literally true, but as an account intended to convey a deeper meaning. We must go behind the words as they are written and come at their meaning in what may be surprising ways. This is like our hunting falcons, which come at their prey in ways which they do not expect. In the same way, we aim to compel the words of the creation story to reveal their deeper meaning.

Master Theodore: And what is the meaning of the account of creation?

Frederick II: I have spoken with Jacob Anatoli and Judah bin Cohen about this. As you know, Jacob Anatoli's family comes from France. He has pointed me to a rabbi named Rashi, who is also from France. Rashi has since died, but many of today's rabbis still look to his teaching.

Master Theodore: And what does this rabbi teach about the creation of the world?

Frederick II: Rashi says, as I understand it, that "scripture did not come to teach the sequence of the creation." He says that if you think it does, with all its numerous contradictions, you should "be astounded at yourself."

Master Theodore: For what reason then does scripture teach the creation account?

Frederick II: Following a rabbi named Isaac, Rashi says that scripture—the Torah which he ascribes to Moses—could very well have begun in the second book. The purpose of the Torah, he says, is to teach the Jews the commandments of god, which are often called the Law. And with a few exceptions in Genesis, these commandments begin in the book of Exodus.

Master Theodore: Why then the creation story?

Frederick II: Here I warm to Rashi. He says that scripture begins "in the beginning" to make clear that he who created the earth is master of the earth and he may give it to whom he pleases. And he chose to give the promised land to the Jews. He says to Abram at Genesis 13:15 "all this land you see, to you I will give it and to your seed forever." He chose to take it away from the Canaanites and the other peoples who lived there and give it to the Jews. What a practical man, this Rashi.

Master Theodore: It is too bad his god could not explain to our departed Pope Gregory that god intends the emperor to rule over all the lands of Italy and Germany.

Frederick II: Yes. As you know, I have visited the holy land myself. I took the cross of a crusader to recover the holy sites of Christendom from the Muslims who had conquered them in 1187. There I accepted the title of king of Jerusalem. But I was not pleased with the land the Jews value so highly. If their god had seen my homeland in Apulia and Sicily, he would not have placed so high a value on the land he gave to the Jews. Nevertheless, this is what Rashi says.

Master Theodore: But there is surely more to the creation story than this.

Frederick II: Yes, but it is confusing and contains many strange assertions. Let me begin with a question which has troubled many philosophers and religious sages. Many Jews—and Christians and Muslims for that matter—believe that god created the world out of nothing, *ex nihilo* as is now said in the Latin church. Before god created the world there was nothing but god. This is a doctrine held tenaciously by priests, rabbis and imams alike, and many who have questioned this view have been denounced as heretics.

Master Theodore: Yes, this is one of the points on which the three monotheisms disagree with Aristotle, who held that the cosmos is eternal.

Frederick II: But consider the words of scripture itself: "Now the earth was astonishingly empty, and darkness was on the face of the deep, and the spirit of god was hovering over the face of the water." Where does this "water" come from and what is this "earth" which is astonishingly empty? Where did these come from? It seems that, despite itself, this account follows one of the deepest thoughts of Greek philosophy.

Master Theodore: What is that?

Frederick II: That nothing can come from nothing. Parmenides spoke to this when he said "it is neither expressible nor thinkable that What-Is-Not, Is. Also, what necessity impelled [Being], if it did spring from Nothing, to be produced later or earlier?" This view is echoed by Melissus and Empedocles. Gorgias said "Being cannot be created." This is also agreed by philosophers like Aristotle, Democritus and Lucretius, who disagree on many other fundamental matters. They all say, as Parmenides said in our language "ex nihilo nihil fit" (nothing comes from nothing). Calcidius says "It is a doctrine common to all philosophers that nothing arises from nothing or passes away into nothing."

There are only two ways in which god might have made the world. One is as an emanation, in which the earth arises directly from the overflowing of god himself. But this is not the view of the creation account The world is not understood as an emanation of god, in which case it would possess god-like qualities itself. No, Master Theodore, the creation of the world is understood as a creative act of god, an act in which god creates something which is new and unlike himself. It may be that humans are created in the image of god, and we shall speak of that, but it is as an image only. Neither humans nor the entirety of creation possess any part of the nature of god.

Master Theodore: If the world is not an emanation of god himself, how then does it come to exist?

Frederick II: It occurs as an act of the will of god. Without this notion of god's will, there is no way to understand the creation of the world.

God wills into being something which is brand new, which did not exist before.

Master Theodore: But can god will something to be out of nothing?

Frederick II: It is said that "nothing … can prove that a thing created from nothing must have been previously in a state of potentiality." But there are many matters which cannot be disproved which do not for that reason become plausible, or even possible. No clear meaning can be attached to the idea of creation from nothing.

Master Theodore: Can we even form a clear idea of not-being? It is both invisible and without qualities or attributes of any kind.

Frederick II: Aristotle hints at the difficulty of this in his metaphysical writings, where he says "we even say that not-being *is* not-being."

Scripture does not say that god created the world out of nothing. Nothing can come from nothing. It is better to say, as I do in the preface to my law code *Liber Augustalis*, god "distributed primal matter." There must be something upon which a creative force acts; it cannot act upon nothing. It is perhaps chaotic and completely without form. It is perhaps totally passive, and exists as pure potential. But somehow there must be something, a substratum of some kind, a potentiality of some kind upon which the act of creation works. Consider a sculptor and a stone. The stone is purely passive. It is a substratum upon which the sculptor works his will. The sculptor is active and the stone is passive. But there still must be a stone to start with. Are not all acts of creation like this?

Master Theodore: Yes, we say that the sculptor is superior to the stone. The sculptor is active and the stone passive. The sculptor actualizes what is only potential before it is actualized.

Frederick II: The stone must exist for its potential to be actualized. An act in which something becomes actual without having first had a potential is not comprehensible to reason. Creation is an act which gives form to what is formless. But there must be some formless substratum of potential—call it what you may—for anything to be created.

One might go further. Some thinkers have wondered whether formlessness or pure matter is simply limitless potential. They have wondered whether matter or formlessness has within itself a tendency to receive forms in different ways. That is, some parts of what is formless, if I could speak that way, carry within them a predilection to receive only certain kinds of forms. The sculptor can make a sculpture out of stone, for example, but not water. That is to say, that which receives must do so in accord with its own potential.

Master Theodore: Shall we prefer one of these views to another? Shall we prefer a wholly formless substratum that can assume whatever qualities its creator gives it, or shall we see this substratum as somehow contributing something to the process of creation?

Frederick II: This is a most difficult question to answer. The main point is that however this formless substratum exists, it cannot be actualized unless it does exist. We cannot comprehend pure creation from nothing. The question remains: why is there this substratum of chaos, of pure potentiality? Why does this exist rather than nothing at all? I do not believe that so long as the world endures, human reason can ever comprehend, much less demonstrate the idea of creation from pure nothingness.

Master Theodore: Is that why the creation account speaks of water and earth and the deep prior to god's creation of the world?

Frederick II: Perhaps so. It seems fair to say that if the creation account in scripture tried to argue for creation from nothing, it did not choose its words well. Perhaps instead it should have said "In the beginning god alone existed." However this may be, it would be a mighty act for a god to create the entire world of forms we see from pure chaos or formlessness. This would be an act worthy of gratitude and worship itself.

Master Theodore: Why then the insistence on creation from nothing? Would it not be sufficient for a faith to be founded upon god's mighty act of creation from the chaotic substratum that must exist?

Frederick II: One would think so. There are two reasons to attribute creation *ex nihilo* to god. One is to attribute a greater power to god than creation from an existing chaos. To see god as less than the sole existent is regarded as a slight against god and a restriction on his will. Creation from something is thought to be less majestic than creation from nothing.

15

It also raises the question of where this pre-existing chaos of pure formless potential could come from. This pre-existing formless potential would have an existence independent of god, and thus possess a dignity of its own. Augustine later tried to solve this problem when he wrote in his *Confessions* that Genesis simply did not mention that god had created the void before he created the earth.

Master Theodore: That seems like a rather large oversight.

Frederick II: Creation from nothing is a doctrine which speaks to the grandeur and purity of a worshipper's view of god, not of anything which is conceivable. And it seems to me that punishing people for failing to believe a doctrine which is impossible to understand does not make much sense.

Master Theodore: This I know reflects your policies as emperor. But let us return to the story. Whether there was a pre-existing potential or whether god alone existed, what does the creation account tell us about how god's creation took place?

Light

Frederick II: God's first creation is said to be light. Scripture says "And God said, 'Let there be light' and there was light." When we say that god's first creation was light, what does this mean? Wise men have suggested that this cannot mean first in a temporal sense because time did not, nor even could yet exist. Time itself, which requires motion or change to be meaningful, arose through the creation of the world. Before that there was no time. Wise men have concluded that perhaps by "first" is meant what comes first in principle, not in time. And perhaps all of creation occurred at once, but was only unfolded over time. Some have likened creation to the planting of seeds all on one day, which then sprout on different following days.

Wise men have also concluded from this that god is not subject to time. He is eternal, not perpetual. That is, he exists not in the sense of a very long time but outside of time altogether. Following Plato in *Timaeus*, the philosopher Boethius says "One thing is certain, fixed by eternal law: nothing that is born can last." William of Auvergne later says most beautifully that to flow in time is to flow into non-being.

Master Theodore: Yes, god could not be subject to generation or corruption and death.

Frederick II: This is held by all religious thinkers.

Master Theodore: What about the world? As a creation of god, is it not then subject to death itself? Will the world one day cease to exist?

Frederick II: There are differing views about this. Some like Basil say that "he who admits a beginning of motion surely does not doubt as to its also having an end." Others point to a passage in scripture in which god promises never to destroy the world. They say god could destroy the world if he wished to, but has decided not to. Still others like Maimonides say that the necessity that what is born must die is true only of things that follow the laws of nature, not those which are created directly by god. This would seem to make the creation of the world different than all other created things. Philo, who seems to follow the Greek philosopher Philolaus, explains it this way. He says that nothing external to the world could destroy the world, because there is nothing external to the whole world. And nothing within the world could destroy it, because that would mean that a part of the whole is stronger than the whole, which cannot be. Thus it is up to god.

Master Theodore: Perhaps it is true that god is the only being external to the world, and if he has decided not to destroy the world, then it will last forever, not subject to an end. But what was god's purpose in creating the world in the first place? He may or may not choose to destroy what he has created, but why did he create it?

Frederick II: This is impossible to know. Religious sages often say the purpose of the world, and humans within it, is to offer worship and glory to god. But this cannot be why god created the world, because he is said to be self-sufficient and in no need of worship or any other thing from his creation. It is rather, as religious sages say, the reason for human beings to worship god is for our sakes, not for god's.

Master Theodore: It seems that everything which is created serves a purpose, but if god—who was not created— has a purpose we cannot know it. God does not speak in scripture about his purpose in creating the world.

Frederick II: Yes, this is a matter of god's will, which even in scripture has not been disclosed to us. When asked his name, god says simply "I am who I am." That is apparently all that can be said.

Master Theodore: This raises a very profound question. As a being which is uncreated, what is the purpose of god's existence?

Frederick II: Yes, a most interesting question. What is uncreated cannot have a purpose. As Maimonides says, we cannot ask the purpose of what has not been created by an agent. We must say according to reason that god's existence has no discernible purpose. It is said that god is uncreated, but simply is. God did not create himself, but simply is. What purpose could be ascribed to such a being? The same is true for Aristotle's cosmos, which he says is eternal. His cosmos cannot have a purpose either. Upon what basis could we say that which is uncreated has an "end?" To say that everything, both what is created by an agent and what exists forever, has an "end" is pure speculation.

Master Theodore: God is a being outside of time, uncreated by anything including himself.

Frederick II: There are great difficulties with the idea of a god who exists within time. Why, for example, would god let time pass and then decide to create the world at a certain moment? What would be god's impulse to do that? There would have to be some impulse. But where could this come from? If god is the eternal, unchanging, sole existing being, from where could such an impulse arise? Not from within god, as he is completely self-sufficient. God requires nothing—not even a created world—to complete him. But neither could it arise from the outside, because it is said there is nothing outside of god. The doctrine of a god who exists in time would have to explain why god created the world when he did and not earlier or later, just as Parmenides said.

Master Theodore: This is fair to say. But why did god choose to create light first among all things?

Frederick II: Here I favor the story. There is no doubt, as we have discussed many times, of the primary importance of light. Light is not merely one of many properties of the world, but perhaps its most important. Of course without light we could not see. But more than that, light is the pre-condition for our ability to discriminate among things. It provides the very possibility of our ability to know anything. God might create the heavens and earth on the following days of creation, but how would we know that if there were no light? You might say, as has one philosopher, that light is the first form of the world. Light is the form which makes all other forms possible, and more than that, possible to know. We should be grateful for light.

The remainder of the creation story stresses the importance of what is separated, what is discriminated, what is set apart. This is the origin of many of the commands of the Law, which are to keep separate what is separate. Light is a good place to begin.

Master Theodore: But what *is* light?

Frederick II: A most excellent—and difficult—question, Master Theodore. Light appears to be an emanation of some kind from certain objects, which in turn makes it possible to recognize objects at all. We cannot see light itself, but only what is illuminated by light. As important as light is, we cannot see it. We can see only the objects which it illuminates.

Master Theodore: What are these emanating objects, and don't they have to pre-exist, or at least exist simultaneously with light? How can light exist before the objects which emanate light?

Frederick II: Another excellent question, Master Theodore. It seems that in the creation account light pre-exists any object from which it emanates. It comes directly from the speech of god, where he says "Let there be light." His speech commands light into existence. Strange to say, but in this account the origin of light has nothing to do with the character of light itself, but arises from speech or sound. But what this light is, where it comes from and what are its pre-conditions is not said.

Master Theodore: Light seems to be a creation from nothing.

Frederick II: Yes, light is the true creation *ex nihilo*. Now one can say there is a god who can do whatever he pleases, without the usual pre-conditions for his actions. Hebrew scholars say, for instance, that the word for god's creation of the world is different than the word to describe human creations. But why should we then liken it in any way to what humans understand as "creating?" These are just so many words, uttered without clear meaning. One might say anything.

Master Theodore: What does Rashi say about this?

Frederick II: Rashi calls the light which god creates the "primordial light." This light pre-exists the creation of the heavens and earth and all the rest of the natural world. This world is not yet created.

Master Theodore: So this primordial light does not come from the sun?

Frederick II: No, Master Theodore. Not at all. The sun has not yet been created. We are familiar with several sources of light—from the sun, the moon and the stars, from lightning, from fire, from auroras and from the glint of steel upon steel which occurs in battle. Each has an object which emits light. Of course the most important source of light is the sun. But neither the sun nor any of these other sources of light with which we are familiar has yet been created.

Master Theodore: So god creates light from nothing?

Frederick II: So it seems. But there is another, deeper question. Did god also create darkness? Or is darkness understood only as an absence, or a privation of light? Is darkness perhaps, as we have discussed, the substratum of pure potential which is necessary for light? Can there be light without darkness?

Master Theodore: Yes, and there is another question. Did god himself live in darkness before he created light? Theologians have often likened god to light, or at least as the source of a kind of illumination. John says at 1: 5-7 that "God is light, and in him is no darkness at all." And Maimonides says of god that "with Him there is no darkness, but the great, strong and permanent light." How does this fit together with the account of creation?

Frederick II: In the creation story darkness pre-existed light, and perhaps is the default state of affairs before god intervenes. This seems clear from the story. Darkness is in a way the pre-existing potential for the creation of light. Without darkness it seems there can be no light. As you have said, religious sages often say that god lives in light, perhaps even that god is light of a certain kind, but that the world was bathed in darkness before it was created. They say further that god rules over both darkness and light, and that he can bring his light to overpower darkness whenever he wills to do so. Same say that god creates darkness as well as light and others that darkness is not opaque to god as it is for humans. Psalm 139 says of god, for example, "even the darkness is not dark to You, the night is as bright as the day; for darkness is as light for You."

Master Theodore: Scripture then says that even without the sun, light is referred to as "day" and darkness as "night" and together they make one day.

Frederick II: This of course is the role which we know the sun plays in creating days. The sun disappears at the end of each day and darkness reasserts itself each night. This suggests the continuing power of darkness to draw the cosmos back into chaos, and to obliterate all that light makes possible. In darkness nothing can be distinguished from anything else. This is why darkness can be so fearful and why we are always grateful to see the light of the sun each morning.

Master Theodore: The creation story takes away this power of the sun?

Frederick II: Yes, Master Theodore, this is exactly the lesson we are to draw. Light is taken away from the sun and given to god. The sun does not create light; both light and the sun are creations of god.

Master Theodore: Scripture then calls the light "good" though darkness is never called good.

Frederick II: Yes, by this is meant not necessarily good for human beings, but good because god achieved what he intended with the creation of light.

But as we have said, light is also good because it allows us to discriminate among the objects in the world. We can with the help of light tell things apart from one another. Without light this would not be possible, or at least not at all easy. Perhaps our other senses could supply some perceptions to us, but without light we would not be able to recognize anything for what it truly is. Our sense of sight, which light makes possible, is truly our most sublime sense.

Blind people can sense what things are only by way of their other senses. But they also have the benefit of what is explained to them by people with sight. Were we a species entirely without sight, we would understand very little of the world in which we live. To give precedence to light, as the creation story does, is surely proper.

Master Theodore: After the creation of light, god creates the heavens and the earth.

Frederick II: Yes, on the second and third days of creation god separates the heavens from the earth and the waters from the land. And on the third day the earth sprouts vegetation, each after its own kind. Imagine that: vegetation sprouts and grows without the sun. We ourselves have done many experiments to show this is not possible. We have light and darkness, the passage of days and nights, and an earth full of vegetation—all without the sun!

Now it is said by some—Avicebron for one—that we should not suppose god needs the sun to make plants grow. This he says would be impudence. Here he agrees with Philo, who said it would be shameless impudence "to attribute to any created thing the primary causes of things." The point is surely that a god one supposes to be all powerful could do as he pleases, unbounded by the limits of human intelligence. One could say anything about a god like this.

Master Theodore: Finally on the fourth day of creation we have the sun.

Frederick II: Yes, on the fourth day god says "Let there be luminaries in the expanse of the heavens." This of course refers to the sun, moon and stars. Especially important are the "two great luminaries" the sun and the moon. These two luminaries are said to rule over the day and night respectively. These luminaries are now given the roles which we know them to have—to separate day and night, to shed light upon the earth, to serve as signs or omens, and to measure the days and seasons and years.

Master Theodore: What happened to the "primordial light?"

Frederick II: There are various views about this. Philo, for example, says the primordial light was perceptible only to the mind, not to the senses. Some say the light came from the sun and moon all along, but they were only suspended in the sky on the fourth day. Rashi says that once the sun and moon were suspended in the sky, the primordial light was "hidden away." It is difficult to imagine where such a light could be hidden. But there is no longer any need for it because the sun and moon now fulfill its task.

Master Theodore: Why then create the primordial light in the first place?

Frederick II: A fair question. Why bother to create a primordial light, only to hide it away in favor of the sun and moon? What could be the reason for this other than to demote the power of the sun in favor of the god of creation?

Master Theodore: The sun is then called the "great luminary" and the moon the "lesser luminary."

Frederick II: This seems fair enough. But these descriptions have become a model—perhaps I should say a pretext—for the popes of our time. Since the time of Gregory VII, popes have looked to the sun and moon as models for human governance. The popes say they have the power of the great luminary, the sun, and the emperor the power of the lesser luminary, the moon. The authors of scripture supposed that the moon was its own source of light, which would have implied the emperor was inferior to the pope. But today, as Innocent III has said publicly, "the moon derives its light from the sun." We know that the moon has no power of its own to illuminate anything. The moon does provide light to the earth at night, but not through its own power. It does so only through the power which it borrows from the sun. And from this the popes of our time have argued at great length that emperors have no power of their own, but only what is granted to them by popes. Innocent IV recently said this: "As the moon receives her light from the more brilliant star, so kings reign by the Chief of the Church who comes from God."

Master Theodore: This seems a convenient model for the popes. Is there any reason to think that popes and emperors can be understood as earthly counterparts to the sun and moon?

Frederick II: You will find no hint of this in scripture. Popes have obviously asserted such a thing to expand the power of the papacy in earthly affairs. But you raise a far deeper question: can the heavens provide a model for human behavior? Can the heavens provide a basis upon which to order human relationships? I will speak more about this later. Here I will say only that although the motives of today's popes are clear, many civilizations have sought to know whether their lives are or should be regulated by the movement of the heavens.

Master Theodore: What then shall we conclude about the creation story?

Frederick II: The principal lesson of the account of creation is to downgrade the importance of the sun. We know the sun as the enabler of the earth and our very being, as well as the pre-condition of our perception and knowledge. The creation story denies this over and over again. The sun is suspended in the sky by a god, who is the true source of light. Neither the earth, nor days and nights nor the vegetation which sprouts on the earth owes anything to the sun. God could just as well take away the sun with no consequence for human life if he chose to do so. He could replace the sun with the primordial light. The sun itself is a creation of god. As Moses says in the Torah, "Take care lest when you lift up your eyes to Heaven and see the sun, the moon and all the stars, you be seduced and drawn away to pay worship and adoration to the creatures which the Lord your God has made for the service of all the nations under Heaven."

Master Theodore: As the philosophers might say, the sun is here demoted to a secondary cause.

Frederick II: Yes, the creation story makes the sun itself a creation of an invisible being. It makes the world a product of a non-corporeal spiritual being who is the primary cause of everything. It points human beings away from the sun which is worshipped by many other peoples and toward the idea of god.

Master Theodore: I see the great pains which this story takes to demote the sun in favor of an idea of god.

Frederick II: When I first heard Flavius Josephus' claim that Plato borrowed many of his doctrines from the older Hebrew accounts I thought this was foolish. But perhaps it is not so foolish. Both describe non-corporeal ideas or spirits which are responsible for the world of which we can have knowledge. Consider the ease with which the Jew Philo and the Christian Augustine suggested that god created a model in his mind before creating the world. There is no hint of this in Genesis, but both thinkers found this an easy way to reconcile Genesis with Plato's *Timaeus*.

Tertullian once asked: "What has Athens to do with Jerusalem?" Perhaps the answer is, more than he understood. Our entire experience with the sun is replicated in the idea of god. Like the sun, we cannot look upon this god directly. And we can know very little of this god, save for what he chooses to reveal to us. And this, I think, is just the point: we cannot know much about this god by reason, but only by what he chooses to reveal to the authors of the creation story.

The Qualities of God

Master Theodore: What then does reason tell us about this god? Who or what is this god and why did he choose to create the world in just the way the story describes?

Frederick II: If you gaze upon the world as it is, and use only your reason, you will not learn very much about such a god, except that god is who or what empowers or is the source of the world. You will not receive any detailed answers to your questions. For more detailed answers you must look to scripture.

Master Theodore: What are these answers?

Frederick II: There are occasions in scripture when god reveals something of himself. But even there far less is said about the nature of god than what god commands the Jews to do. And we cannot force god to reveal himself with our questions. He reveals what he wishes, when he wishes. God makes his wishes known to the Jews from time to time. It seems that he speaks directly to Moses and a handful of others and indirectly to the rest of the Jews.

Master Theodore: Does this god really "speak" to humans? Is he really "angry" when the Jews disobey his commands? Could this be true?

Frederick II: It does seem strange, doesn't it, that humans would have such an ability to control the emotions of an all-powerful god, or that such a god should even have emotions. But wise men have looked at all this very differently. They look at scripture from the standpoint of philosophy. Philo of Alexandria, whom I have already mentioned, writes this way. Philo looks at scripture through the eyes of Greek philosophy, especially Plato, and aims to translate the words of scripture into the language of philosophy.

Master Theodore: How does he do this?

Frederick II: He does this by treating scripture as an allegory. He says the true meaning of scripture is better understood in this way.

Master Theodore: Do the Jews accept this?

Frederick II: As I said, Philo is not much known among the Jews of today. Rabbis prefer to focus directly on the words of scripture and not to go behind them with another tradition, so to speak, to discover a deeper meaning. But we do not need to look to the distant past to find Jewish thinkers who aim to reconcile scripture with Greek philosophy. We have in our own time the best and deepest Jewish thinker who does this.

Master Theodore: You refer of course to Maimonides.

Frederick II: Yes, the most excellent Maimonides. No one has better aimed to reconcile Jewish scripture with philosophy. Maimonides is the fullest fruit of our age in which this is possible. Maimonides borrows from the Arabic tradition, relying heavily upon the Muslim philosopher we know as Averroes. His great work *The Guide for the Perplexed* was written in Arabic. Jacob Anatoli's father-in-law Samuel ibn Tibbon translated many of Maimonides' works, including the *Guide*, from Arabic into Hebrew. Maimonides can be critical of Averroes, but he owes much to him.

Master Theodore: Yes, you have commissioned translations of Averroes and Maimonides in order to make their work more widely available to the Latin-speaking west. Together Jacob Anatoli and Michael Scot have translated portions of Maimonides' *Guide* from Arabic into Latin. What is your understanding of Maimonides' teaching about Jewish scripture?

Frederick II: He begins with a very important statement. Listen well to this: Maimonides quotes favorably the Talmudic saying "the Torah speaks the language of man."

Master Theodore: What is his meaning?

Frederick II: The Torah, he says, was given to the Jews in order that everyone could understand it. It is written in a way such that all people, even those not much endowed with intellect or inclined to philosophy, can understand it. It speaks of the Jewish god as if he were a very powerful human being, with all the qualities and passions of a human being. This god is angry or displeased, just as are human beings. And he reveals his wishes in speaking and in actions much as would any human being. His messages are meant to be understood by the masses.

Master Theodore: Yes, I see your point. But what has this to do with reason or Greek philosophy?

Frederick II: Maimonides says that the speeches and commands of god must be understood allegorically. God does not actually speak, as if he had a voice like a human being. This would be to give god material qualities like a tongue, which he surely does not have. All statements of this sort—where god "says" or "speaks" or "commands"—must be taken as figures, not literally. God may communicate with human beings, but if he does, he does so in a manner all his own. But these commands must somehow be understandable to human beings. All descriptions of god "speaking" to man, if they are taken literally, are insults to the majesty of god. They reduce god to a kind of super-human being, replete with a body, organs of speech and human passions.

Master Theodore: Is this true of the creation story as well?

Frederick II: Yes. God never "breathed" life into Adam, for god has no breath. He has no lungs with which to breathe. God cannot truly be known so long as people believe this sort of thing. Philosophy teaches that god has no attributes at all, human or otherwise. An attribute, as the philosophers say, is an "accident" and god can have no accidental qualities. Any quality which god may have must be understood as necessary; indeed, Maimonides says it is a mistake to attribute qualities to god at all. We men know god from his actions, which we wrongly take to be god's qualities. To try to understand god by giving him human qualities leads one further from, not closer to god.

Master Theodore: This is very radical.

Frederick II: Maimonides goes further. He says that we humans— even when we wish to worship god sincerely and obediently—cannot do so adequately if we are worshipping a god with human qualities. We are far from god when we do this. Nor do we properly give god human names. Maimonides says, for example, that when we call god "lord" we are using an analogy to the way in which we are obedient to an earthly ruler. All the names we give to god are appellations drawn from human experience. There is only one name for god which is not and that is the tetragrammaton, the Hebrew letters yod, he, vau, he, which we render as YHWH, a name which is not regularly to be written or spoken. It is to recognize that this name, this X as the Arabic teachers of algebra might say, is beyond human ability to comprehend or to name properly.

Master Theodore: This is a very abstract, even distant god.

Frederick II: Maimonides speaks to this directly. He says there is no such thing as "nearness" to god. God does not exist in a particular place, such as do all material things. If god exists at all, he surely exists everywhere and nowhere. Speaking of growing "nearer" to god is an allegory drawn from human participation in the material world. When we truly know god—that is as a non-corporeal spiritual being, with our mind—we are no "nearer" to him at all. This is just a manner of speaking.

Master Theodore: This is a very common way of speaking.

Frederick II: Yes, but philosophers and religious thinkers like Maimonides are clear. They say god cannot be perceived by or known through the senses at all. The senses can perceive only what is sens-ible. What is sensible must exist in a time and a place, so god cannot be a sens-ible being. He can be truly known only through the mind, but even then largely only negatively. He can be known by the mind as a being without time or place, everywhere and nowhere. This of course does not tell us anything very specific about god, only that he exists in such a way that our human understanding cannot fully comprehend. We can approach knowledge of god only through negative predicates. Maimonides says the more negative predicates we give to god, the closer we are to knowing him. When we cast aside our limited human ideas about god, we know him better.

Philosophy teaches that god exists, that he is non-corporeal, and that his essence and existence are implied in one another, as the Arab philosophers might say; this is the demonstrably certain knowledge of god that Maimonides grants to reason. In this way through means of philosophy we can comprehend that god's non-corporeal, unchangeable nature makes him utterly different than the world which he has created. We must learn "there is no similarity in any way whatsoever between

Him and his creatures." Philosophy cannot teach us much about god, but it teaches all that can be known with certainty about him.

Master Theodore: This seems to provide a very limited knowledge about god. Are there no other ways we can obtain knowledge about god?

Frederick II: Here there is great irony. The creator is said to be far above, and very much unlike, his creation. But philosophers and religious sages then say that it is only through what god has created—the world—that we can have any specific knowledge about him at all. Having depreciated the sun and all other parts of creation, it turns out that this very creation offers to our reason the only clues about what god is like. Philo, for example, says that our knowledge ascends from the earth to the heavens and finally to the one who has created the heavens and the earth. He says that in this way a wise man can "form a conjectural conception of the Creator by a probable train of reasoning." And Maimonides, who has said there is no similarity between god and his creation, then says "we can only obtain a knowledge of Him from his works." For example, if we see order and beauty in the creation, we might infer that god is an admirer of order and beauty.

Master Theodore: So we can have some knowledge of god from the world in which we live?

Frederick II: It seems this is the only way to have specific knowledge about god, and it is very inferential at that. It is as if we have only the sculpture in front of us with which to know the sculptor. As usual Maimonides puts this very clearly. He says that we cannot rightly compare the creation with the creator. But then he says we can know a little about god by studying his creation.

Master Theodore: It is ironic that having depreciated the creation vis-à-vis the creator, the creation is nevertheless the only way to learn about god by reason.

Frederick II: In one sense this is of course true; if god had not created the world and humans within it we would be unable to know anything at all about god. But the only way we can know about the spiritual, non-corporeal god is by studying his creation. As Maimonides says, we can learn about god only through his actions or works. Other than the several demonstrative truths about god, reflection on the world is the proper way in which god is sought by wise men.

Master Theodore: It seems that diligent study is required to know anything at all about god and thus about how to worship him properly.

Frederick II: Yes, so it would seem.

Master Theodore: What can this study teach us about how we are to live? Can we receive instructions from this study to tell us that?

Ethics

Frederick II: Maimonides, along with most Christian and many Muslim philosophers, asserts that we can gain knowledge about the created world. They say, of course, that god is the primary cause of everything. But they say that god has chosen to structure the world in an orderly way that can be known by human reason. This structure is a world governed by regular secondary causes. This is what we aim to learn through philosophy or science. Such knowledge comes in two forms. The first is what can be known directly and with certainty through logical deductions from first premises. The other is the slower, less certain—but still real—knowledge that comes through observation. These are often referred to as demonstrative and observational forms of knowledge. My book on hunting with falcons is of the latter type, where I aim to show things as they truly are.

Master Theodore: Do these secondary causes then constrain god himself?

Frederick II: An excellent question, Master Theodore. Many arguments have arisen over this simple question. I shall speak about it in more detail when we discuss Islam, where it occupies a central place. I would say here only that thinkers of all three monotheistic faiths argue that god is free to suspend the regular working of secondary causes. This suspension is what is called a miracle. But note, too, that the idea of a miracle implies some notion of the regular working of secondary causes. How else would we know that these secondary causes had been suspended? What would be miraculous without a regular order of things against which it is juxtaposed?

Master Theodore: Is god then free to do whatever he pleases? Is nothing impossible for god?

Frederick II: Some theologians have said god is free to do anything at all. Others, who are more thoughtful, have said god cannot do what is impossible. For example, can god make a square whose diagonal is equal in length to one of its sides? It seems this would be impossible, even for god. Those who favor god's perfect freedom might respond that it is only our limited human comprehension which makes this impossible. But there are even harder questions. Can god create another being exactly like himself? Can god choose to destroy himself? Those who argue that nothing is impossible for god have no good answers to these questions.

Master Theodore: Let us assume then we can have genuine knowledge of the orderly workings of the created world. This seems to me to raise two very difficult questions. One is whether we humans too are part of the regularly operating secondary causes. That is, do we humans have free will or are our actions shaped by the secondary causes that shape the rest of creation? And second, if we are not shaped by these secondary causes, but have free will, does the study of the heavens teach us anything at all about how we should live?

Frederick II: Excellent questions both, Master Theodore. Many views have been offered about whether our actions are shaped by secondary causes. No faith seems able to say this is entirely the case, and still argue that we deserve (at least in any humanly understandable way) a fate which awaits us. To argue that god shapes our behavior in advance is to suggest that we are not free to do good or to sin of our own volition. Yet every faith exhorts us to do what is good and to shun what is evil as if we are free to make such choices ourselves.

Moreover, if we are free to act on our own, does this not suggest some limit to god's power? In this way, god would not be the creator of all that occurs. We shall see this thought in the Muslim philosopher al-Ghazali.

Master Theodore: Yes, it seems that all teaching, instruction and exhortation, and all of our laws as well, suppose that humans have some latitude to make their own choices.

Frederick II: To address this dilemma thinkers of each theological tradition have proposed complex and subtle arguments. Some have involved arguments that god is outside of time and others have argued that freedom and determinism are two sides of the same coin. All these arguments strike me as valiant attempts which fall far short of being persuasive. To reconcile god's omnipotence and human free will seems an impossible task.

Master Theodore: Yes, it seems so. Let us suppose that humans have some freedom of the will. Can the regularly occurring secondary causes of the world—the stars, as some might say—teach us how we are to live?

Frederick II: In *Timaeus* Plato suggests that human behavior is to some extent influenced by, and should be shaped according to the model of the cosmic forces that move the stars. He says that learning about the cosmos can offer both theoretical and practical knowledge. He says that knowledge of the stars provides a model for our political life.

Master Theodore: Does Plato actually believe this?

Frederick II: It is hard to say. After all, Plato offers these thoughts through the mouth of a participant in the dialogue and calls them a "probable account."

Master Theodore: Does Plato say how far knowledge of the stars is useful and what are its limits?

Frederick II: Not in so many words.

Master Theodore: Do the religious sages follow Plato's thinking about the stars?

Frederick II: No. The three monotheistic religions are very skeptical that the stars can shape our behavior. They allow for knowledge of the movement of the stars, but are very suspicious of any view that impinges on human free will. They do not favor any view that says humans should model their acts on the movement of the stars. After all, if it were possible to gain this knowledge through reason, why would we need the revelations of scripture? Why would we need rabbis, the church and its priests, or imams?

Master Theodore: Yes, it seems that Hebrew scripture contains many warnings against those who favor astral power.

Frederick II: This is true from the very beginning of the Torah. In Genesis we have the story of the serpent who tempts Adam and Eve. Let us not suppose there was actually a talking serpent; let us attend to what this story is trying to teach us. What is the tree from which god forbade Adam and Eve to eat? It is the tree which offers knowledge of good and evil. In seeking knowledge of good and evil, Adam and Eve were seeking to be god-like. Seeking knowledge of good and evil by reason alone is to aim to be like god. Only god has this knowledge. Adam and Eve are punished by god for this act.

Master Theodore: Only god then defines what is good and what is evil?

Frederick II: Yes. We cannot attain knowledge of what is good and evil by human reason alone. By eating of the tree, Adam and Eve learned that which they had not known previously: the very act of disobeying god is the essence of evil. There is no way to reason our way to knowledge of good and evil. Reason cannot teach us ethics. Only by following god's commands as they are set out in scripture can we learn what is good. As is said in Hebrew scripture, the fear of god is the beginning of wisdom. As might also be said, for scripture it is also the end of wisdom.

Mater Theodore: Is this also the lesson of the tower of Babel?

Frederick II: Yes, these people were trying to build a tower to reach to the heavens. They were seeking the knowledge of the stars. And god destroyed this project, which was an attempt to raise humans to the level of god.

Master Theodore: What does Maimonides say about this?

Frederick II: Maimonides believes we can understand the regular workings of creation. But he does not believe that knowledge of secondary causes, no matter how complete, can teach us how we are to live. He draws a distinction between the first and second commandments received from Moses and the third to tenth commandments. The first two, he says, speak to the existence of god and can be learned from natural reason as well as from revelation. The other eight commandments cannot be known by reason and require the revelation of scripture.

Master Theodore: The first two commandments are, in a manner of speaking, between man and god; the other eight are between man and man.

Frederick II: Yes, the last eight commandments Maimonides calls "ethical and authoritative." These commandments do not contain truths which are perceived directly by the intellect. Our knowledge of the regularly occurring secondary causes within creation does not teach us how to live. There can be no certain knowledge of morality. Maimonides calls morality a "science of apparent truths."

Master Theodore: Maimonides does not then reject philosophy or science?

Frederick II: Not at all. But he rejects the notion that we can derive rules for human behavior from such knowledge. He speaks again and again of the Sabeans, who stand for peoples who worshipped the stars or the heavens and who sought to derive rules for human behavior from them. He says that despite their many rituals, they attained no knowledge of morality. They were full of human impudence and were like the men who wished to create a tower reaching to the heavens.

Master Theodore: The Sabeans sound very much like the Chaldeans in the writing of Philo.

Frederick II: Yes, Philo sees the Chaldeans in very much the same way. They were a people filled up with the claims of knowledge; like the Sabeans they aimed to use their knowledge of the creation to learn how humans should live. And Philo says this is exactly what distinguished Abram from the Chaldeans among whom he lived; Abram was the first to turn his back on the claim that reason can teach us how to live. This can be known only by worshipping the true god, not the idols created by human reason.

Master Theodore: Yes, Abram is said to be the first man to teach the meaning of one god rather than the idols of man.

Frederick II: The Jewish tradition rejects ethics based upon human reason; it turns away from a reason-based ethic in favor of worshipping a god who provides an ethic through his commands. Maimonides says pointedly that the world does not exist for man's sake.

Master Theodore: What does he mean?

Frederick II: By this he means the world was not constructed in such a way that we humans can know our place and know how to live on our own, as it were, through our reason alone. We require the continuing commands of god in order to live well. Human reason, even if it attains a complete knowledge of the stars, cannot tell us how to live. The universe does not speak to us about morality at all. We might say, as does scripture, that the heavens declare the glory of god. But the heavens do not offer us guidance about how to live.

Master Theodore: Without knowledge of ethics, how are we to live?

The Law

Frederick II: This is the purpose of what the Jews call the Law. The Law consists of the commands of god. Maimonides follows the standard identification of 613 commands in all.

Master Theodore: Where are these found?

Frederick II: They do not come from reason or nature. They are revealed in the first five books of scripture. They are precepts commanded by god and written down in scripture by those who received them.

Master Theodore: Isn't there a problem with this?

Frederick II: What is that?

Master Theodore: When god "speaks" a command, this must not be understood literally but allegorically. Aren't all the commands of god found in allegorical form? Isn't this a weak basis on which to rest god's commands and the precepts the Jews are to follow?

Frederick II: Here we must distinguish between the means by which the commands are received—which are allegorical—and the content of those commands which the Jews take literally. In this way there is no difference between a wise man who understands the allegories and the mass of men who do not; the commands are binding on both.

Master Theodore: These commands seem to cover all aspects of life, leaving very little human behavior which is not addressed.

Frederick II: Yes, they cover sacrifices and other rites, care of the body, human emissions, hair, dress, sexual relations and the everyday dealings of men. They are a comprehensive set of commands about how the Jews are to live.

Master Theodore: Does god really care about all these matters? What difference could it make to a self-sufficient, all-powerful god how the Jews wear their hair?

Frederick II: A fair question. These laws are surely an extra burden on the Jews and one might fairly wonder why god puts these additional burdens on them. Peter Abelard's philosopher, for example, argues that these precepts are neither necessary nor useful. Unlike the simpler Christian rules, namely, to love god and one's neighbor, the Jews are under the heavy burden of the Law. And as Abelard's philosopher says, following the commands of god does not even offer to the Jews the benefit of eternal life.

Master Theodore: Is there a reason for these commands? Do they serve useful human ends? Or are they purely arbitrary—a matter of god's will? Do they serve a purpose which humans can understand?

Frederick II: Maimonides speaks to this. He says there are good reasons for the commands of god. God's commands are not purely arbitrary. They serve important human purposes. The Jews of today may not know why each and every command exists, but on the whole the commands serve humanly useful purposes. This Maimonides says is surely true of the broader commands, if not of every detailed command. For example, animals are to be eaten for human sustenance, but why it matters if the animals are killed from the front or the back of the neck is less clear.

Master Theodore: Is there an overriding purpose to the commands?

Frederick II: Maimonides says there are two broad purposes: to guide the Jews in their worship of the one true god and to regulate the relationships between men. Of these the former is more important.

Master Theodore: In what way do the commands guide the Jews to worship god properly?

Frederick II: The overriding purpose of the Law is to counteract the temptation to idolatry. Most of the details of the commands can be understood in this way. They are meant to command the Jews to do things differently than their neighbors who were considered to be idolaters. If the Canaanites, the Sabeans, the Chaldeans or the Egyptians did things in one way, the Jews are invariably commanded to do things in a different way. If the idolaters created graven images, the Jews are not to do so. Maimonides goes so far as to say this is why Abraham established the west side of the temple as most holy. It is because the idolaters who worshipped the sun believed the east, where the sun rises each day, is most holy. Many of the commands of god can be understood in just this way.

Master Theodore: Does this not demonstrate that these commands were the product of a specific time, in which the Jews were trying to establish their worship of god? Have they any relevance to Jews in the 13th century?

Frederick II: For the Jews some of the temptations of idolatry are a permanent part of the human condition. It is the permanent temptation of idolatry to worship something of god's creation rather than god himself. But Maimonides admits that other commands do speak mainly to their own time. Indeed, Maimonides suggests that some of the commands make use of the practices of the Jews' neighbors at the time they were issued. He suggests that god was gradually trying to wean the Jews away from the practices of their neighbors. We might suppose, for example, there is less purpose today to the commands relating to the proper way in which to offer animal sacrifices.

Master Theodore: One could then say of the commandments of the Law that they arose from the attempt to set the Jews apart from other peoples and to separate the Jews as a unique people who worship their god.

Frederick II: Yes, that would be fair to say. And it is the reason why other peoples of ancient times thought the Jews were insular and unlike all other peoples.

Master Theodore: In what way are the relations of men with one another addressed in the Law?

Frederick II: There are many commandments which speak to the ways in which Jews are to treat one another, and even strangers. These commands constitute a significant portion of the Law.

Master Theodore: This is what we would call morality or ethics.

Frederick II: Yes, the Jews derive their ethical code from the Law. The precepts of their moral code are not founded in reason or nature, but in tradition, that is, following the commands of god as they are revealed in scripture. There is nothing in nature, for example, that teaches us we should have only one wife. The Muslims follow another practice. My friend al-Kamil among the Egyptians is married to many women. It has been my practice to follow the customs of the Muslims in this regard. A rule to have only one wife cannot be found in nature; if found anywhere, it can be found only in the commands of scripture.

Master Theodore: Are the moral commands of scripture also then reasonable or are they arbitrary?

Frederick II: There is a degree of arbitrariness in them, as the differing practices of the three monotheistic faiths make clear. Maimonides says, however, that the moral commands of scripture are broadly reasonable and understandable. They aim to create and maintain healthy, clean bodies and they aim to promote harmony or justice among men. Maimonides says that "the Law, though not a product of Nature, is nevertheless not entirely foreign to Nature."

Master Theodore: Does Maimonides then put human notions of harmony and justice as the arbiters of whether these commands are "reasonable?"

Frederick II: Yes, that is fair to say. His point is that as commands of god they are to be obeyed, however reasonable or unreasonable they may seem to us. But he says there is "wisdom" in these commands and that there is therefore human utility in obeying them. It is not so much that the Law contradicts anything derived from reason as that it goes beyond what reason can teach us.

Master Theodore: Are some of the commands of the Law more important than others, or are they all equal?

Frederick II: The ones which speak against idolatry are the most important. Maimonides says the commandments regarding property are important. But commands regarding the body are even more important. And commands involving one's character are more important yet. But the commands which lead to a proper worship of god are the most important of all.

Master Theodore: How do the Jews know that what is said in scripture is a genuine command of god and not a false command of men? Isn't all of scripture what you have often called "hearsay?"

Frederick II: At one point in scripture this question is addressed. It says there that one can tell who is a true prophet, and not a false one, by whether their prophecies come true.

Master Theodore: This is not too helpful in the moment.

Frederick II: Fair enough. Belief that scripture contains the true commands of god presupposes belief in those who claim to receive these commands directly from god. Belief in the Law presupposes a belief in prophecy, that is, that some men have heard directly from god and that these men are to be believed. For the Jews this is true above all for their greatest prophet, Moses.

Master Theodore: How do the Jews know Moses was a true prophet and not a false prophet?

Frederick II: Here the wisest man is on the same ground as the mass of men. The wisest man can form a deeper, truer notion of god than can the mass of men. Human reason can lead wise men away from the false impressions of god held by the masses. But no matter how much closer to the true worship of god is a wise man, he must defer to the prophets. For wise men have no independent, reasoned basis for understanding the commands of god which are the Law. That is why it is called the Law; it is not to be questioned by reason, but obeyed as the product of prophets who have heard directly from god. Prophets surpass even wise men; they have the power of both reason and revelation.

Master Theodore: So for the Jews prophets stand above wise men?

Frederick II: Yes.

Master Theodore: To what then can wise men aspire?

Frederick II: One thing above all. Wise men cannot reason their way to morality. But living by the moral code of revelation is said to assist wise men in their quest for wisdom. A wise man who lives by the code of the Law will gain the stable temperament necessary to become wiser. A wise man thus will be aided in his use of reason. Reason proposes there must be some ground or cause or reason why the world exists. To reflect upon this is the highest use of human reason. For religious sages this means to seek to know god. For a Greek philosopher like Plato it is to reflect upon being and what makes intellection of the world possible. How, and why, does the world exist at all?

To undertake this kind of thinking is the fullest use of our reason. As Boethius says, "This power, whatever it may be, by which created things are sustained and kept in motion, I call by the name which all men use, God."

Master Theodore: So for the Jews morality does not derive from reason, but the path of reason is made smoother by morality.

Frederick II: Well said, Master Theodore. For those of us who are not prophets, a life devoted to understanding the source of all being and of the world is the highest possible task. Maimonides says many years of study are necessary. He says that one cannot rush into this subject, but must come to it through long and careful preparation. For ancient Greeks this perhaps meant to be initiated into secret rites which laid out a path toward wisdom. For Maimonides and the Jewish sages it meant withholding the secrets of this study until a listener is prepared to understand them. But however it is described it comes to the same thing: to achieve an intellectual understanding of first things, of primary causes, of the reason there is being at all. So the increase of wisdom rests upon a life of moral character; reason does not teach morality, morality assists reason. We will never reason our way to all the commands of morality. Rather, morality opens a path on which only a few wise men are likely to travel, that is, to a life which displays moderation in earthly practices combined with a dedication to the highest truths. This is not a path on which many men will tread and it is certainly no basis upon which to found a government to rule over the mass of men.

ON CHRISTIANITY

Frederick II: Let us speak now of Christianity, our own faith in the Latin west.

The History of the Church

Master Theodore: Is this a new faith or an extension of Judaism, about which we have spoken?

Frederick II: An excellent question, Master Theodore. It is both. The bishops of the early church held widely divergent views about this. Those from early Jewish-Christian congregations saw Christianity as an outgrowth of Judaism. Those further from Jerusalem—in Asia Minor, Greece and Rome—saw less need for a close connection between Judaism and Christianity. Impassioned arguments occurred about whether the Jewish Law must be followed by Christians, and especially whether a Christian must be circumcised.

Mater Theodore: This was not resolved for many years.

Frederick II: As late as the second century Marcion and his followers argued that Christianity was a definite break with Judaism. The loving god of Christianity, he said, is very different and far superior to the jealous, vengeful tribal god of the Jews. And lest one think Marcion was a marginal figure, he was the first of many bishops to draw up a canon of the books which came to be called the New Testament.

Master Theodore: But he was anathematized for his views, was he not?

Frederick II: Yes. Marcion stimulated a broad attack on his views. The dominant view of the Christian bishops at the time, expressed most clearly by Justin Martyr, said that Christianity was the fulfillment of god's promise to the Jews. He said that god did not change his mind about his promises, but that the Jews did not understand their true meaning. This view was echoed by Clement, Irenaeus, Tertullian, Origen, Augustine and many other important bishops. In this they followed Paul, who himself had been a Jew before his conversion. Paul was the first to say that the promises to Abraham pointed to Jesus. In doing so, of course, he had to de-emphasize the idea that god's promises were made to Abraham's "seed." Paul's Christianity was rooted in the Hebrew scriptures, but since he was mainly speaking to gentile audiences he argued there was no need for Christians to follow all the laws of the Jews.

Master Theodore: How did they argue that Jesus was the messiah whom god had promised in the Jewish scriptures?

Frederick II: They found support for this view not only from Paul's letters but from Matthew, who wrote what you might call the most Jewish of the gospels. There Matthew has Jesus say that he did not come to abolish the Law but to fulfill it. But much more than this was required. Proponents of this view combed through the Hebrew scriptures to find evidence that Jesus was the promised messiah. This often required Hebrew scriptures to be read allegorically. Eusebius went so far as to say that the names "Jesus" and "Christ" were well known to Moses, Jacob, Joshua and later to Isaiah and David. He said these Jews were Christians in fact, if not in name. He also observed that even more ancient figures—including Adam, Noah and Abraham himself—did not follow the Law because the Law was not yet given. The Law was not given until Moses. So following the Law cannot be the most decisive part of knowing god. These were very creative acts of interpretation; many passages were read allegorically in ways that seem far from their authors' intentions. And of course the Jews do not accept this.

Master Theodore: But the Jews themselves have occasionally adopted allegorical readings of their own scriptures.

Frederick II: Yes, as we have discussed. Philo read the Hebrew scriptures allegorically. But it was not to demonstrate that these scriptures pointed to Jesus but to demonstrate their consistency with

Greek philosophy. And as we also discussed earlier, in our own time Maimonides has done so in a very deep way. But the Jews do not read their scriptures as pointing to Jesus.

Master Theodore: It was settled, then, that for Christians the Hebrew scriptures constitute an old testament which belongs together with the new.

Frederick II: Yes, that question has been settled since the middle of the second century.

Master Theodore: With this issue settled, has there been continuity in church doctrine and practices since the second century?

Frederick II: There has been continuity, but also many changes. Most of these changes have been for the worse. Our popes today—and I think especially of our recently departed Gregory—pretend that today's church doctrines and practices are the same as those of the earliest church. This they pretend even as they are busy changing both church doctrines and practices. Their view is convenient but it is not true. Popes who have taken the name Gregory, including Gregory IX, often seem to have been those most eager to expand the earthly power and wealth of the church.

Master Theodore: What changes have they made?

Frederick II: They have elevated the bishop of Rome far above other bishops, calling him since the time of Damasus I the father of the church. They have reorganized to their own advantage the process of papal selection. They now wear a red mantle to distinguish themselves from mere cardinals of the church. Bishops now turn their backs to the congregation when they receive holy communion. They have become ever more insistent about the strange doctrine that the body and blood of Jesus are actually present during the eucharist. They have made this doctrine binding only as recently as three decades ago in the Lateran Council of 1215. And in recent years they have made up the new notion of purgatory, about which there is no reference either in the scriptures or the traditions of the church.

Mater Theodore: Their reasons for this are apparent.

Frederick II: Yes, they aim to aggrandize both the wealth and power of popes. For this the notion of purgatory is a very convenient tool; many souls which are destined to ascend to heaven one day are said to suffer the cleansing fire of purgatory—but their suffering can be conveniently shortened by payments to the church.

Popes plot against emperors and claim not only spiritual power but the power to enter into political alliances like other kings. They now assert they have the power not only to name emperors but also to depose them. None of these doctrines can be found in the early Christian church.

Master Theodore: From where do popes say they receive their authority?

Frederick II: They assert that it comes directly from god, though one would look in vain in the writings of the early church to find any evidence of this. Worse yet, they pretend to amass their wealth and power in the name of the emperor Constantine. They say Constantine gave these powers to popes. But the so-called Donation of Constantine cannot be credited. The Constantine I have studied, and whose role I have emulated, would have done no such thing.

Master Theodore: Are not the crusades another example?

Frederick II: This is well said, Master Theodore. The intention to recover the holy lands for Christianity is fair enough. Muslims have no natural right to control the holy lands which they have acquired by conquest. What claim to the holy lands do Muslims have to which Christians do not have a better claim? And to be fair, the Jews have the best claim of all. The holy lands have been taken by force by Muslim armies. Is there any reason they should not be taken back by force? Should Christians not have the right to visit Bethlehem, which means nothing to the followers of Muhammad?

Beneath the public veneer of the crusades, however, are to be found less noble motives. Popes levy onerous taxes on their subjects to pay for the crusades, but much of this money stays in Rome to be used as popes may please. And wily popes speak of a duty which lies upon emperors to take the cross and regain control of the holy lands. There is no scriptural basis for this claim, which is often made only to weaken the power of emperors. I resisted going on crusade as long as I could. I knew that in my absence the pope would scheme to consolidate his power over my territory. And this, which was very easy to foresee, was exactly what happened. As soon as I departed for Jerusalem the pope stirred up trouble in my empire. I had to rush home to defend what for me was far more important than the re-conquest of the holy lands. I was able to achieve by negotiating with al-Kamil a ten year truce, during which Christians regained the right to travel to Jerusalem and Bethlehem, along with a corridor to the sea. In this way I accomplished far more, and at far less cost, than my crusading predecessors in 1202 and 1221, not to speak of the ill-fated children's crusade in 1212.

Tell me, Master Theodore, what these actions have to do with the true spiritual role of the church. I have spoken about this with Francis of Assisi, who also traveled to Egypt to meet with al-Kamil about the holy lands. He has offered a much needed reminder to the church of what should be its pure and simple spirituality.

Master Theodore: Many changes have occurred since the earliest days of the church. What accounts for these changes?

Frederick II: My answer is simple: Roman emperors and Greek philosophy. Let us speak first of Roman emperors.

Master Theodore: We must speak about Constantine.

Frederick II: Yes, my distant predecessor, the great emperor Constantine. Before he became sole emperor, many religions existed side by side in the empire, some Christian and some pagan. The number of Christians had been increasing year by year despite—some might say because of—the waves of persecution which they bravely endured. Constantine's predecessor Diocletian was of two minds about persecution; nevertheless he allowed persecution to run rampant, especially in the east. It appeared to Constantine that the persecution of Christians was a failure, producing the opposite of its intended effect. Constantine brought the persecution of Christians to an end. In its place he established a policy of toleration. The Edict of Milan which he and co-emperor Licinius propounded granted to all citizens "the free choice of following whatever form of worship they please." Constantine said this edict was intended to foster peacefulness in the empire.

Master Theodore: This has been your policy as well.

Frederick II: Yes, I have learned from Constantine. I make it a point to tolerate each of the faiths in my empire—Christians, Jews and Muslims alike. So long as these faiths do not disturb the peace or challenge my rule I see no point to persecute them.

Master Theodore: Did Constantine adopt this policy because he was a believing Christian or because it suited his imperial rule?

Frederick II: It is difficult to read the hearts of men, especially many years distant from us. We can reasonably doubt the legends which grew up about his victory at the Milvian Bridge, many of which were spread by his only-sometimes-truthful biographer Eusebius. Many of the emperor's pronouncements which Eusebius took to be expressions of the Christian faith were rather general in nature. Constantine often referred to "one god," but this and other formulations would have offended no one. But there is no doubt that Constantine took many actions designed to help Christian churches in the empire, and he was baptized just prior to his death in 337. It is perhaps enough to say that both spiritual and practical ends pointed him in the same direction.

Master Theodore: Was his policy of toleration effective?

Frederick II: Yes, to a point. It brought the large and growing number of Christians into the imperial orbit and gave them a stake in Constantine's policies. As I will explain further, however, this blessing has also been the source of many harmful changes within Christianity. Christians entered into the politics of the empire and later became almost synonymous with the empire itself. Christians have departed entirely from the sound advice of Eusebius who said that the bishops of the church "should once for all be kept absolutely free from all public offices." Constantine rightly said that when bishops render service to god they confer in this way incalculable service to the state.

Master Theodore: Constantine also discovered there were many disagreements among Christians.

Frederick II: Yes, Constantine said there were no more disputatious people in the empire than Christians themselves.

Master Theodore: About what did the Christians dispute?

Frederick II: Nearly everything. The succession of bishops, the rules of baptism, the purity of bishops, the proper date on which to celebrate

Easter, the status of Jesus' mother Mary—these and many other matters separated Christians from one another. But the deepest and most persistent differences concerned the nature of Jesus himself.

Master Theodore: How did Constantine address these matters?

Frederick II: He did not want differences between Christians to threaten the peace of the empire. He was convinced that a unified Christian view on matters of doctrine and practice was critical to the welfare of the empire. Wherever he could, he urged bishops to resolve differences between themselves. In these disputes he cared less about the details of the outcome than that there be agreement.

Master Theodore: There were disputes which the bishops were unable to resolve among themselves.

Frederick II: Yes. On several occasions he convened the bishops himself. The Council of Nicaea in 325 was the most important of these occasions. This was the very first ecumenical Christian council and it established a precedent; until the eighth century every ecumenical Christian council was convened not by the church but by emperors. As was said about the Council of Constantinople in 551, for example, "we assembled here by the will of god and the command of the emperor."

Master Theodore: Did the Council at Nicaea achieve agreement among the bishops?

Frederick II: Yes and no. Constantine pressed the several hundred bishops gathered at Nicaea to adopt an agreed creed of the church. This creed was modified afterward on several occasions but it did establish an official church position. But many of the issues that led to the Council persisted and were revisited later by Constantine himself.

Master Theodore: Constantine seems not to have concerned himself about the doctrines which were in dispute.

Frederick II: The dispute concerned whether Jesus was of one substance with god or of a lesser substance. Bishops Alexander and Arias argued passionately for their positions. I will say more of this later. Constantine thought these differences were "intrinsically trifling and of little moment." He was exasperated with the bishops' constant strife over what he called "trifling and foolish verbal differences." He urged the bishops to put aside their arcane views, about which nothing can be known in any event. If bishops were not able to do so, Constantine said they should at least confine their differences "to the secret custody of their own minds and thoughts."

Master Theodore: It seems that Constantine sought Christian unity for its own sake and not on behalf of his own view of the nature of Jesus.

Frederick II: Constantine sided with Alexander against Arias, no doubt because Alexander held the majority view. But in the end it was Constantine who compelled the outcome at the Council of Nicaea.

Master Theodore: Did this effort succeed in unifying church doctrine?

Frederick II: Not entirely, but well enough. Constantine was able to secure the support of the vast majority of the bishops to create an official church doctrine. In doing so he offered gifts and favorable tax treatment to bishops who supported the Nicene Creed. But the Council did not succeed in making Arias or his followers disappear. This was in part because Arias had many good arguments, some from the mouth of Jesus himself. In due time Constantine made his own peace with Arias. Doctrinal disputes have surfaced over and over, often around the same issues that were debated at Nicaea. We see hints of this among the Cathars today.

Master Theodore: What happened after Constantine's death in 337?

Frederick II: Subsequent emperors adopted differing policies. Julian, who became known as the apostate, turned away from Christianity and toward traditional Roman gods. But by then Christianity had established itself as the dominant faith in the empire. It did not take very long before Emperor Theodosius established in 380 not only spiritual but also temporal penalties against non-Christians. In a mere sixty-five years Roman emperors went from persecuting Christianity to tolerating it to enforcing it.

Master Theodore: In the following years the empire itself was split into two parts. In the east, governed from the city which Constantine named after himself, emperors continued to play a role in shaping Christian doctrine and practices. But the imperial city of Rome was disastrously weakened and the power of western emperors dwindled to nothing.

Frederick II: In the absence of imperial leadership the bishops of Rome grew far stronger. The bishop of Rome, who had not even attended the Council of Nicaea, became the undisputed leader of the church. Popes stepped happily into the vacuum of imperial leadership. The eastern empire had split off, invaders from the north repeatedly occupied Rome and the former Roman territories in northern Africa and even Spain were conquered by the Muslims. The empire was far smaller, but what remained came increasingly under the sway of the popes and the church.

Master Theodore: Speak about the emperor Justinian.

Frederick II: Justinian illustrates this well. He made a valiant effort to restore the Roman empire. But he was also the enforcer of the doctrines of the church. In 529 he began to persecute non-Christians. Among other acts, he closed the school which traced its lineage all the way back to Plato's academy in Athens. Many of the philosophers there relocated to the lands of the Arabs and the Persians, who were more welcoming to them than was the Christian west. Perhaps this is one reason why Arabs grappled sooner and more deeply with the relationship between their faith and Aristotle's philosophy.

Master Theodore: There is no doubt that Christianity was the dominant force in the west for many centuries. There was no other unifying force in the western empire.

Frederick II: Yes, this was true until the time of Charles, who is rightly called Charles the Great. He was strong enough to try to resurrect the former imperial glory of Rome, though on a different basis. The result was a new Christian version of the old Roman empire. Charles exercised considerable power in his own right, but he allowed himself to be crowned emperor by the pope, which the pope took as a sign of his superiority over the emperor. Charles is rightly called the first Holy Roman Emperor, a title which future emperors including myself have held.

Master Theodore: Charles' successors were not strong enough to exercise independent power. As emperors came and went, they often struggled against popes who by now sought not only spiritual power but temporal power as well.

Frederick II: What you say is true. From the time of Charles, popes and emperors have struggled against one another. Charles' father Pepin took the fateful step of granting to the pope temporal as well as spiritual power in the region around Rome we now call the Papal States. Though this seemed a useful, perhaps even necessary step at the time, it created long-lasting conflicts between popes and emperors. The popes of today know no bounds to their lust for temporal as well as spiritual power. Where they can rule directly, they do so; where they cannot, they forge alliances against the emperor. I have confronted the most aggressive, ambitious and avaricious popes in the history of the church.

Master Theodore: You confront these forces each day.

Frederick II: Today's popes have inverted the order of the ancient Roman empire. Then popes were confirmed, sometimes even appointed by emperors. Now popes claim the power not only to appoint but also to depose emperors.

Master Theodore: They use all the powers of their office to do this.

Frederick II: Yes, in addition to their wealth they have one other powerful tool: the threat of excommunication. This threat terrifies the ignorant. As you know, I have been excommunicated three times. This has had little effect on me, as popes rescind their judgments against me whenever they think I can be of use. Excommunication is a political tool masquerading as a spiritual power.

Master Theodore: Popes have opposed at every turn your legitimate powers as emperor.

Frederick II: Yes, this has been very difficult for me. But as I have said, this lust for temporal power has also been harmful to the church itself. Today's popes have taken the church very far from its original simple spirituality. Popes now expect emperors to do their bidding, including enforcing their judgments against heretics. I will act swiftly against heretics if I deem them a threat to my rule. This is surely not in doubt, as I have demonstrated. But it should be for the church to define heresy and for the emperor to determine what he will and will not enforce. The emperor should not be a handmaiden to the popes of Rome.

Master Theodore: The history of the church has been closely bound up with that of Roman emperors. You have well said how emperors once helped to define the practices, and even the doctrines, of the church. We have come a long way from those days.

We have spoken mainly of the ways popes have wrongly claimed temporal power. Speak now about the role of Greek philosophy in regard to the doctrines of the church.

Christian Doctrine

Frederick II: You are correct to speak of Christian doctrine. The Jews have the Law, but a doctrine or dogma is very different. It is not a law which is to be obeyed, but a set of beliefs which are to be accepted. There is a great difference in this way between Judaism and Christianity.

Master Theodore: The doctrines taken on faith are central to Christianity.

Frederick II: Yes, Master Theodore. It is in the struggle over these doctrines that ancient Greek philosophy enters. Christianity rests upon the person of Jesus and his resurrection. But the notion of bodily resurrection is fundamentally at odds with Greek philosophy.

Master Theodore: Explain this.

Frederick II: Let me begin by saying that like Philo and Maimonides, Christian theologians have confronted Greek philosophy. They have asked what can be known of god by natural reason. Natural reason teaches that god is a spiritual substance, everywhere and nowhere. It teaches that god exists as the creator of all there is, but that he himself is not bound by time and place as would be a material or bodily substance. This the church fathers accept. They say that god does not have a body but is a spirit. They stated at the Lateran Council of 1215 that while god's unlikeness to humans is far greater than his likeness, it is not to the point of abolishing our language and the use of analogies to describe god. There is much Greek philosophy in all this.

Master Theodore: What then is different?

Frederick II: Now comes Jesus, a human being in a place and a time. Jesus does not come as a spirit but rather, as the church fathers insist, as a real human being who can suffer like other human beings. How can this be said of a god?

51

Master Theodore: Such an idea has the great advantage to bring the distant god of philosophy and of the Jews down to earth. It puts a human face on god which god never had for the Jews and which of course the philosophers deny.

Frederick II: The god of the Jews never shows his face to human beings. Jesus brings to human beings a face of god which for thoughtful Jews like Maimonides and philosophers can be known only through negative predicates. This is the role of Jesus—to be god incarnate, in a place and time and able to be comprehended by the senses. Jews heard the voice of god only through burning bushes and other contrivances, and apparently their god is no longer speaking in even these ways. Jesus makes knowing god directly far easier for the mass of people.

Master Theodore: This gives Christianity a genuine popular appeal.

Frederick II: Yes, Master Theodore, but it also raises very deep questions. Let us consider first place, or location in space. Jesus was born and lived in Judea. Why did god come there? Why did he not come to Rome or someplace else? This cannot be known by reason and must be accepted on faith.

Moreover, when Jesus died it is said that he "ascended" to heaven. As I am fond to ask of scholars, where is heaven? Is it "above" the earth, suggesting that it is a place or a location? Is heaven to be found in a "place" in the cosmos? Do Christians speak accurately when they say that people can "go" to heaven, much like one can travel to Judea or Rome? If god is a spirit, as all serious Christian thinkers say, how can he reside in a physical place called heaven? Wise men say that heaven has no other place than in the mind of god.

Master Theodore: Christians say that not only Jesus, but all believers will "go" to heaven.

Frederick II: Yes, but as Augustine, Basil, Abelard and others have said, human beings cannot draw "near" to god as one could draw near to another body. They say that nearness to god must be understood as a figure which means close to god not in space, but in morals or merit. So too with the idea of "sitting at the right hand of god." No one actually sits there; god does not have hands.

Master Theodore: Most Christians do not think this way.

Frederick II: For most Christians who are not troubled by philosophy heaven is thought to be a place somewhere. This must be so because where else could bodies be, except in a place somewhere? If Christians are to be resurrected bodily, how could this be otherwise? This is just what is meant by body: what is sprit is not body and what is body is not spirit. When Paul speaks of "spiritual bodes" he utters words with no meaning at all. Sprits are nowhere and everywhere, bodies are somewhere.

Master Theodore: It seems that Christians give the afterlife a more tangible existence than do the Jews.

Frederick II: The Jews do speak of a "place" called Sheol, which is said to be "down" but it does not play a very big role in Jewish thought. The Pharisees also taught about resurrection and an afterlife but they have since disappeared. As Abelard has said, Jews do not gain a happy afterlife by following their Law, but receive whatever rewards there are in this life.

Master Theodore: Most Christians also believe there is a "place" called hell.

Frederick II: Yes, but Jesus did not speak much about it. Many early Christians did not think there was a place called hell. They thought that non-believers would not "go" to a place called hell but simply die and not enjoy the happy afterlife of heaven. Only Matthew speaks much about hell and Paul never refers to it in his letters. But the main body of Christian bishops rejected the spiritualizing tendency of Greek philosophy, especially as it presented itself in gnosticism. Over time hell took on more physical characteristics and became a "place" to which non-believers "go." It even became official church doctrine that Jesus himself "descended" into hell for three days, though there is only one hint of this in the scriptures. In First Peter 3:19 it says that Jesus "went and preached to the spirits in prison," which is nowhere mentioned in the reports of the gospels. You will find no mention of hell in either the Nicene Creed of 325 or the Creed agreed at Constantinople in 381.

Master Theodore: And in recent years the church has created a third "place" in the afterlife, the idea of purgatory about which we have spoken.

Frederick II: Yes, the idea of purgation has become for the church a "place" called purgatory. Nowhere does scripture speak of such a place.

Master Theodore: Jesus lived at a certain time in history as well.

Frederick II: Yes, he was born during the reign of Augustus. He was born, he grew and he died—all in human time. As we have said, church fathers who knew Greek philosophy say that god exists outside of time altogether. It is only our inability to know everything at once that causes humans to think within the divisions of time called past, present and future. For god there is no human time—for god all that is, as they say, is *tota simul.*

Master Theodore: And then comes Jesus, a god who exists within time. How is this possible?

Frederick II: Just as one might ask of a god within time why he chose to create the world when he did, and not sooner or later, one could ask this about Jesus as well. Why did he come when he did, and not earlier or later? Why just then? This too cannot be answered.

Master Theodore: It seems very difficult to reconcile a spirit god who is outside of time and space with a god who lived within time and space.

Frederick II: Yes, this has been the central dispute within Christianity: how to understand the relation between god and Jesus. Many views have been expressed, the easiest to understand of course being that Jesus was a human being and no part of god at all. This view, however, was outside the pale of Christian thinking from its very earliest days. What Christians disputed among themselves was the relation between god and Jesus. Is Jesus a "part" of god the father, even though only material beings can have "parts?" Is he an emanation of god or a part of god himself? Is he an equal part of god? Did he exist from all time as part of god and assume a human form only temporarily?

Master Theodore: Jesus referred to god as his father.

Frederick II: Yes, but what he meant is uncertain. Is this a figure or is it to be taken literally? There are many places in scripture, to which Arias pointed, that suggest Jesus thought god was superior to himself. All the questions I have asked arose as church fathers responded to the questions of Greek philosophy.

Master Theodore: This was the meaning of the dispute with Arias.

Frederick II: Yes, it concerned the arcane question of whether Jesus was of a different and lesser "substance" or of the same substance as god. In 325 the church fathers declared that Jesus was of the same substance as god, using the Greek word *homoousios*. As they said twice in the creed of 325, Jesus was "of one substance with the Father." Unless one believes that the church fathers at Nicaea were every bit as inspired as the gospel writers, there is no reason to subscribe to this addition to the simple words of Jesus. To me this doctrine looks less like inspiration than a dispute settled in the way regular quarrels are settled. This is just the way I came to agreement with al-Kamil about the future of Jerusalem.

Master Theodore: The creed is an agreed formula but its meaning is far from clear.

Frederick II: Yes, the church fathers said that Jesus was "begotten not made." What does this mean? It is directed against the Arian view that god created Jesus in the same manner he creates anything else in the universe. But how does the word "begotten" resolve this question? Children are "begotten" by their parents, and so share their nature. This much is clear. But whoever is begotten comes after the parents and is not with them before they are begotten. The creed anathematizes those who say there was a time when Jesus was not and who say that before being born, Jesus was not. These are words addressing matters which cannot be known and upon which little matters in practice.

Master Theodore: This is a church doctrine that goes beyond the words of scripture. If this were not enough, the church also then speaks of a third and equal "part" of god, namely, the holy spirit.

Frederick II: Yes, this makes matters more complex. In the gospel of John, which you might call the most Greek of the gospels, John has Jesus say that he will send assistance to those who believe in him. So far as I can see, nowhere is this assistance ever described, and it is certainly not elevated to be a third "part" of god.

Master Theodore: How was this doctrine of the three parts of god developed?

Frederick II: The holy spirit was mentioned in the creed of 325, but was given little significance. It is only in the years after 325 that church fathers developed the doctrine of a holy spirit as an equal part of god, and on slim scriptural evidence at that. The holy spirit is called by John a *paraclete,* which means advocate or helper. But who or what is this helper? Is not god himself a spirit? When the holy spirit acts, is this not just god himself acting by filling people with his spirit? Is the holy spirit the spirit of a spirit, which has no meaning? Is it not better understood simply as the spirit of god in action? Basil, for example, says that the spirit which was hovering over the waters in the beginning of the world was the holy spirit. He and the other Cappodocian fathers are the ones most responsible for elevating the holy spirit to an equal part of god.

Master Theodore: This doctrine seems complex.

Frederick II: After 325 many Christian bishops turned away from the Creed of 325, preferring to think of Jesus as "like" the father *(homoios,* as the Greeks say) rather than of identical substance with the father. But in turn this view was reversed and by the time of Theodosius the Nicene Creed was re-established as official church doctrine. The creed of 381 speaks of a holy spirit who is "the Lord and life-giver" who "proceeds" from god and together is worshipped with the father and the son.

Master Theodore: This is thenceforth known as the trinity.

Frederick II: Yes. Is there any place in scripture in which the trinity is a genuine teaching of Jesus? The entire notion of the trinity seems clearly modeled on the philosopher Plotinus' notion of the One, *nous* or *logos*, and the world soul. Nearly all church fathers agree that we cannot derive the idea of the trinity from natural reason, but neither can it be easily derived from scripture.

Master Theodore: Christian doctrine does not speak of god in three parts, but as god in three "persons."

Frederick II: If there is one thing which god, Jesus and the holy spirit are not, it is a "person." This is certainly true of god and the holy spirit, who can in no meaningful way be thought of as persons. Never before the Cappodocian fathers was such a thing heard of. We have here ever deeper obscurity. To defend this compromise between a monotheistic god and polytheism, Christian church fathers said that the trinity is a "mystery" which must be accepted not because Jesus spoke of it but because the church insists upon it. They say that only the father knows how Jesus was "begotten."

Master Theodore: The holy spirit is said to be co-substantial with god from all time. Yet the creed of 381, which has become the official creed of the church, speaks of the holy spirit as "proceeding" from god. What does this mean?

Frederick II: That is a fair question. The word "proceed" seems to suggest the opposite of what is intended, namely, that the holy spirit is an emanation of god and not co-equal with god. After all, the holy spirit is sent by god, which seems to imply that god is above the holy spirit in importance. And the later church made this no clearer when it adopted a new doctrine, namely, that the holy spirit "proceeded" from both god and the son. This view was rejected by the eastern church and remains one of the principal reasons why the Roman church and the eastern church remain separate. Imagine what Constantine would have thought about centuries of division over the one word *filioque*.

Master Theodore: There is contained within the notion of a holy spirit another idea which was foreign to the Jews. That is the idea that god sends help to individuals who believe the Christian doctrines.

Frederick II: This is a very wise observation, Master Theodore. When god sends help to individuals it is often called by the church "grace." It is said to be unearned. This we do not see in the same way in Judaism. In Judaism god creates a covenant with the Jewish people, not with individual believers. This covenant is a kind of deal or treaty, much like we might make with an ally. When the Jews follow the Law they prosper; when they do not they are punished. It is true there are times when a just god would have given up on the Jews altogether. But the Jewish god does not, and he remains faithful to the Jews even when they disobey the Law. This I suppose could be called a kind of grace as well. But as for individuals like Noah and Abraham, they are rewarded by god for their goodness and loyalty; they earn it in the manner of Abraham who demonstrated his willingness to sacrifice his son. But since the Law was given by Moses, god's grace—if one may call it that—operates for the whole of the Jewish people.

Master Theodore: Grace is extended to individuals in Christianity.

Frederick II: Yes. Like the Hebrew god, the Christian god decides when he will and will not extend grace. But for Christians grace is offered to help individuals through difficult challenges or to mark them for salvation.

Master Theodore: This in turn raises a major question for Christianity. Can individuals earn god's grace?

Frederick II: If Christians cannot earn grace why should they bother to try? But if they can merit god's grace, why was it necessary for Jesus to die on the cross?

Will

Master Theodore: The idea of grace is founded upon god's will. God may choose to grant grace or to withhold it.

Frederick II: The Hebrew god may grant or withhold his favor as well, but it is not the same. When the Hebrew god wills, he displays his power. This power of course is an act of god's will, but the emphasis is on god's power or efficacy. This we see in the talks between Moses and the pharaoh; Yahweh demonstrates that his power is greater than that of the Egyptian gods.

Master Theodore: How does this differ in Christianity?

Frederick II: For Christianity god's will expresses itself through god's actions, but the emphasis is on god's will itself, rather than on its display of power. God's omnipotence is displayed through the acts of his will. Today's Christian thinkers derive some of their emphasis on god's will from their reading of Arabic scholars like Avicenna.

Master Theodore: What is "will?"

Frederick II: Will is the ability to make different what is. When god wills, he makes things different than they would otherwise be. Basil, for example, says that god needed "only the impulse of his will to bring the immensities of the visible world into being." In our own time William of Auvergne speaks of god's will when he says that "nothing comes from [god] except through his will." God's essence is equivalent to his will.

Master Theodore: How does god express his will? It is said that he does through his "word." Does god actually speak words?

Frederick II: No, Master Theodore, the "word" of god is a figure. God's "word" is not expressed in the way in which the vulgar believe. Basil, for example, says that god has no voice with which to utter a word, for god has no tongue. The "word" is a way to describe the will of god so that humans might understand it. William of Auvergne says that god creates by speaking a word, but this word is not audible or perceptual. It is a spiritual word.

Master Theodore: God's word then is a kind of thought.

Frederick II: So it seems for the most thoughtful Christians, Master Theodore. God's will is expressed in his thought, which is called a word so it might be more easily understood. When humans have a thought, nothing in the outside world changes; when god has a thought, the thought itself brings about change. This is the difference between god and humans.

Master Theodore: Humans do not issue commands with their thoughts but with their words. Their thoughts alone cannot change anything.

Frederick II: Yes, I issue commands by the sound of my voice, not by my thoughts.

Master Theodore: If humans are to understand the commands of god they must be expressed in words.

Frederick II: You have touched upon a very deep matter here. It concerns the difference between seeing and hearing, between light and sound.

Master Theodore: Please explain your meaning.

Frederick II: I will explain this more fully later. But for now we might say that with sight one sees what is. One sees the truth of things as they reveal themselves, or are revealed to us. With sight that is enabled by light, one sees the truth of beings directly. There is no compulsion here, beyond what must be admitted by the self-evidence of things.

Master Theodore: How are hearing and sound different?

Frederick II: We do not hear the truth of things directly. We do not learn directly from sound. Sound (a word) is the basis for command, for rule. As Maimonides points out, the Hebrew word *shama* means "to hear" but also "to obey." This is a kind of external compulsion.

Master Theodore: From where comes the "truth" of what is commanded?

Frederick II: It must be based on an original seeing of some kind. But if there is an original seeing of some kind, why can't we all see for ourselves? Sight is given to all. When we see the truth of something we say we are "enlightened" not "ensounded." We might say that one learns from sight and one teaches through sound. It is through hearing that obedience, guilt and morals arise.

Master Theodore: It is through the "word" that god is said to express his will. Is god's will unlimited or is it bounded in some way?

Frederick II: The vulgar say that god's will is omnipotent, meaning there are no bounds to god's will. But so too do many Christian thinkers, including even those who have been influenced by philosophy. John Philoponus, for example, says god does not need pre-existing substance to create. God can create matter and form at the same time; he says god's "mere willing suffices to give substance to things." Gregory of Nyssa says it is a deep mystery how the material, compound and extended world can be created by a god who is immaterial, simple and without extension. Peter Damian goes so far as to suggest in *On divine Omnipotence* that god can restore virginity to a woman who has lost it. This of course is to suggest that god can undo what has happened in the past, a past which he has entirely foreseen. And William of Auvergne says god "acts without the possibility of being in any way prevented from doing what he wishes or being forced to do what he does not wish." God's will is perfectly free, which is the same as saying that god is omnipotent.

Master Theodore: Is god omnipotent? Can he do anything?

Frederick II: Those who answer in the affirmative do so for one reason: they say that although god is simply one, he can create more than one. Arabic philosophers like Avicenna have argued that what is simply one can emanate only one thing. This Christians deny, saying that even though god is simply one, he can create through his will as many things as he wishes.

Master Theodore: Is there nothing that god cannot do?

Frederick II: We have discussed this with regard to Hebrew scripture.. For Christians it is much the same. It is only to say here that in Christianity we find even more emphasis on the unlimited nature of god's will. For the Jews it is important that Yahweh is more powerful than any other god. For Christians this is insufficiently reverent; god's will must be unbounded and where we cannot understand how this is so, it is because it passes all human understanding.

Master Theodore: If god's will has no bounds, can god create evil?

Frederick II: This is a very difficult question, to which Christians have offered many differing answers. Some say that god does not create evil, leaving the question of whether he could do so to the side. They say that he created Satan good, but that Satan "fell" into evil himself. Others like Abelard say that god can and does create evil, but always uses evil for the good.

Master Theodore: It remains a question that if god can create anything he wishes, why does he allow evil (even if he did not create it) to exist in the world? Why did god not create a world with no possibility of evil? What is to be gained for an omnipotent god to create a world with evil in it? Why would god do such a thing if he could will it otherwise?

Frederick II: A fair question, Master Theodore. Let me say this: if there is no evil, how can we know there is good? Must not evil exist for the idea of good to be understandable? For there to be any meaning in the idea that god is good, there must be some notion of what is not good, or of that which is evil.

Master Theodore: Is an omnipotent will free?

Frederick II: A very deep question, Master Theodore, which is another way of speaking about whether god is able to do any and all things he wills. An omnipotent will that is compelled to do good seems at first blush not to be fully free. A will which is free is one that could will to do anything or its opposite. This is what it means to be free, to have a choice. What else could freedom of the will mean? We do not say a stone rolls downhill or that water flows downhill because they will to do so. This would be to suggest that the stone or the water have some choice in the matter. But the stone and the water do not have such a choice. To be able to do otherwise is what it seems to mean for a will to be free.

Master Theodore: Shall we say then that god could create evil but that he does not choose to do so?

Frederick II: We can obtain some knowledge about what god chooses to do only by observing what god has in fact chosen to do. How could we know what else god might or might not be able to do? We can assert what we wish about such a god, but we can know nothing about this. For this reason many Christians say that god is good because there is good in the world or even that that world is ordered in a wonderful way. But then comes again the question of disorder and evil.

Master Theodore: Most Christians say that god is good in his very nature and that he necessarily wills what is good.

Frederick II: Yes, they suggest that goodness is not a choice of god but is a part of god's very being; it is not an "accident" added to god's essence. They say that god does not act randomly or capriciously but according to his own necessity. By this is meant that his will is free because he does not act under any external compulsion, but only according to his own nature.

Our word "good" is what is for us highest and most important, and we wish to ascribe to god the fullness of that virtue. This cannot be known by reason, but must be learned from what prophets relate to us through direct revelations from god. My own opinion is this: when we look out at the world, we can see much beauty and an order which is understandable to us. This suggests that a god who has created this world favors beauty and order. But it does not explain very well the existence of disorder and evil, which also exist, and it certainly not does speak to the question whether god has the power to have created a different world altogether. We can draw such conclusions only from mere speculation.

Master Theodore: Are Christianity, Judaism and Islam of the same view?

Frederick II: All assert that god is good and merciful, but beyond these assertions there are great differences. The god of the Jews does what is good for the people he favors, although this goodness does not always look good to non-Jews, or sometimes even to the Jews themselves. The Christian god is said to be and to do good, and it is asserted that this is intrinsic to his essence or being. For Muslims it is different yet. For them god is said to be good and merciful, but these human words cannot bind god's completely free will. For Muslims god does not do what is good, but what god does is what is good. We shall speak more of this later.

Reason

Master Theodore: What makes possible the choices which are set before a free will?

Frederick II: This is the role of reason.

Master Theodore: What is reason?

Frederick II: Reason is the capacity to see what is, what is similar and what is different. It can then work backward and forward according to clear rules, to ask how differences and similarities exist and what are the consequences of each.

Master Theodore: Do Christians believe god is omnipotent and his will is free because he has reason, which puts the fullness of choices before him?

Frederick II: It is said that this is so, but only upon analogy with human will and reason. Christians say that god, his reason and his will necessarily aim toward the good. It is not clear whether such a god has the fullness of options before him or whether he somehow acts necessarily through his very nature to do what is good. This cannot be known, but only asserted. Does god think like we do? Does he think about himself? The most thoughtful authors have said that god's reason bears little relation to human reason because much about god is unknowable.

Master Theodore: Do Christians believe that human beings have reason and free will?

Frederick II: For Christians human beings are essentially willing beings. Reason does indeed put choices before the will. Where there is no reason there can be no will. But reason cannot choose anything itself. It is only a kind of adviser or counselor to the will, which is the most important quality of a human being. This is very different than the view of Greek philosophers, who said that human reason is perfectly capable of choosing.

Master Theodore: Are humans then capable of willing freely?

Frederick II: Yes, to a point. Our wills are not as free as god's will. There are limits to what we can will, many of which arise from our having bodies. We cannot choose to fly like our falcons. But human beings, endowed with reason and will do have a capacity to choose, especially in the most important way: to turn toward god or away from god.

Master Theodore: Reason and will speak to our similarity to god.

Frederick II: Long ago Boethius described humans this way: "you, made in the likeness of god by virtue of your reason." Basil says this is what is meant when scripture speaks of man as created "in god's image." Being created in god's image does not refer to our bodily shape. God is a spirit which does not look like a flesh and blood human being. Basil says that god has no body and therefore no shape of which human beings could be an image. He says "in god's image" means that we share important qualities of god, although in a lesser way. Chief among these are our will and our reason.

Master Theodore: Scripture uses a plural form at Genesis 1:26, saying that god said he would make men "in *our* image." What is meant by this?

Frederick II: Maimonides says that god consulted with his angels before he made men, though it is difficult to think he really believes this. Christian theologians have said that this confirms that god exists in three persons.

Master Theodore: But the will is always pre-eminent in men.

Frederick II: Yes, reason is only a counselor which makes known various options for the will. For Greek philosophers we always will the good, reasoning to discover what is truly and most fully good. For Christians we can will good or evil, and without god's aid it seems more often we will evil.

Master Theodore: Can humans reason too much?

Frederick II: Many influential Christians say this is possible. Reason can ponder questions which take us further, and not closer to a simple faith in god. As Basil said, "Let us Christians prefer the simplicity of our faith to the demonstrations of human reason." As others have said, reason can be a snare of delusion. The task for a Christian is not to reason his way to the truth, but for his will to believe.

Master Theodore: Humans then have freedom of the will, at least for the most important question of salvation. How do they reconcile god's omnipotence with human free will?

Frederick II: This is an insoluble problem. Many clever authors have tried to explain this, but as I have said, never with success. It is the same for philosophers who try to reconcile atomistic determinism with human free will. It seems that neither the existence of free will nor its opposite—whether understood as god's omnipotence or atomic determinism—can be demonstrated by reason. If god provides grace to some, where is their choice? If god does not, where is their choice? All that can be said is that this is a mystery which passes human understanding. We shall see this issue even more starkly when we discuss the Muslim faith.

Master Theodore: Though will is dominant, reason is still important.

Frederick II: Yes, without reason we can have no conception of god at all. The proof of this is that animals do not have a conception of god.

Master Theodore: As we have discussed, there cannot be one without the other.

Frederick II: Reason plays a smaller role than the will in believing, as we see in the scriptures. But in our own time reason has become more and more important. Christian thinkers have aimed to conform reason with faith and to learn how far reason can take us toward an understanding of god. They say that a claim is not "unbelievable" if it goes beyond reason, but only if it contradicts reason. Reason is becoming more of a standard today by which to measure the claims of faith.

Master Theodore: What can reason teach us about the world?

Frederick II: Christian thinkers today say that reason can teach us much about what are called secondary causes. While god lies behind all as the primary cause, they say that unaided reason can teach us much that is true and useful. Reason follows the rules of thinking which we call logic, which produces knowledge which is demonstrably true. Reason also can discern patterns in how the world operates and test these notions against experience. This is what I aim to do in my book on falconry. I have followed only reason and experience, without slavishly relying on ancient authorities or revelation.

Master Theodore: You ascribe to nature, and never directly to god, the causes of the types and activities of hunting birds.

Frederick II: We observe that secondary causes follow patterns which we can discern. One could say this is due to the primary cause of god which makes them how they are and not otherwise. But this assertion takes us no further toward knowledge of secondary causes. These must be discovered by reason and experience.

Master Theodore: Do we discover knowledge through what Augustine calls god's "illumination?"

Frederick II: Here is where Aristotle is important. Today's Christian thinkers—Abelard, William of Auvergne, Robert Grosseteste (who has unhelpfully sided with the pope against me recently), our own Albert, choose who you may—all say god lies behind all things. But they say that reason and experience can teach us what is true and useful. For them reason has become a far stronger, more trustworthy faculty. One may say that god created human reason, but if he did, it is reason and not the speculations about god which we call metaphysics or theology which teach us about the world. In this manner god's continuing illumination is thought to be neither necessary nor helpful to learn about the things of the world.

Master Theodore: Perhaps god has made both the world and our reason in such a way that we can understand the world.

Frederick II: One can say this. But however it came to be, our reason is both necessary and sufficient to learn about the things of the world. We do not have to be illuminated by god at every step of the way.

Master Theodore: The world is ordered in a regular, unvarying way, such that we can understand its workings.

Frederick II: Yes, the causes of things often operate in a regular, orderly way. William of Auvergne says that natural causes do not operate randomly or of their own volition; he says that natural causes operate in the nature of a servant. God seems not to intervene regularly in either the secondary causes of things or in providing us with illumination about these matters.

Master Theodore: This has caused Christian thinkers to ask not only what we can know of secondary causes, but of the three-fold god which lies behind them. What does reason teach us about this god and what depends upon the texts of revelation?

Frederick II: If I may summarize their conclusions, they are these: reason teaches us there is a god, faith in revelation teaches us about Jesus, and the holy spirit is a mystery that cannot be comprehended by either reason or faith.

Master Theodore: Reason has its own realm in which it operates without the constant intervention or illumination by god.

Frederick II: Yes, the rules of thought, or logic, are known directly by our reason. Aristotle taught that the simple concepts we use are known directly by reason, without demonstration or illumination. They are neither true nor false, but are accepted by us as self-evident. They are known directly by human reason. That is why they are held in common by thinkers of all faiths, no matter what other revelations their faiths accept. There is no active role for god here; reason teaches us directly and by it we come to have knowledge of things as they are.

Master Theodore: One might say god lies behind all this as a primary cause of everything, but god is not necessary to reason about simple truths or more complex truths. These are known directly by reason, and are tested by experience.

Frederick II: That is well said, Master Theodore. We have no need for revelation to teach us either simple truths or more complex truths about the world.

Master Theodore: Is everything about the world open to reason?

Frederick II: Another very deep question, Master Theodore. We might say that in principle there is no reason why this should not be so. We do not know how far our reason extends, as this is something we find out only by experience. The most interesting question for reason in our time concerns whether we can make predictions about the future based upon our knowledge of the world.

Master Theodore: People have always relied on predictions, have they not? People predict it will be colder in winter and take steps to prepare for that.

Frederick II: This is true. What I am referring to is astrology, the study of the stars and the planets and the ways in which these bodies affect human beings.

Master Theodore: Why would we think these bodies influence human beings and their decisions?

Frederick II: As we have discussed, these have been questions since the beginning of Greek philosophy. Plato spoke of the stars and planets as en-souled as are human beings. Their souls accounted for their movements through the skies. Can one say in principle that these movements in no way affect human beings and their choices? The world examined by astrologers is a cosmos in which humans live and operate, naturally affecting and being affected by the rest of the cosmos. Can one rule out that the movement of the stars and planets has some effect on human beings? Could we not learn something about how to predict outcomes from such a study?

Master Theodore: What do Christians think about this?

Frederick II: Christians are very skeptical about, often deeply opposed to astrology. This is so for several reasons. Most important is that the possibility of predicting human behavior by the study of the stars leaves no room for the Christian idea of free will. If human outcomes can be predicted by such knowledge, where is free choice?

Master Theodore: This is why Christians also oppose the philosophy of atomistic determinism. If the future can be known in advance, this seems to deny the existence of free will. The predictability of the future—whether through the idea of god's omnipotence or through atomistic determinism—runs counter to the free will attributed to human beings.

Frederick II: There is another reason. If humans can predict the future through knowledge of the stars, why do we need the church and its revelations? This kind of knowledge leads inevitably to worship of the world, which Christians oppose.

Master Theodore: This is also opposed by the Jews and the Muslims.

Frederick II: Yes, this is the cardinal sin for all three religions—to worship the things of the world as opposed to the spirit which is god. But there is another reason to distrust astrology.

Master Theodore: What is that?

Frederick II: Astrology seems to produce very little knowledge which is of clear use. Astrologers take refuge in vague sayings and predictions which can be found out to be true no matter what outcomes occur. It has yet to prove its worth in a practical way.

Master Theodore: But you consult astrologers, do you not?

Frederick II: Yes, I see nothing to lose. But I do not put too much trust in them because they do not seem to produce much that is of use. I tested one of my astrologers in this very way. He said the distance between a star and a church in my realm was of a certain length. Unknown to him, I razed the church and rebuilt it at a different elevation. He was able to detect the difference, meaning that the movement of the stars can be measured. But this does not prove their effects on human choices.

Master Theodore: Is there a parallel between astral and human life? Should humans be aligned, if that is the correct word, with the astral world?

Frederick II: My view is that it depends upon what knowledge, if any, arises from the study of the stars. To this point I see no reason to see a parallel between the movements of the stars and human choices.

Master Theodore: The predictions of astrologers, so far as they are clearly said, seem no better than the predictions anyone might make. But there is another form of knowledge which reason seeks and that is what is called after the Arabic word "alchemy." Is knowledge of this sort possible?

Frederick II: Alchemy is the attempt to change what exists from one form to another. I see no reason in principle why this should not be possible. Something—one may say god—has made the forms of what exists. They did not arise from nowhere, but rather they are as they are because of the way in which they assumed their forms. As Augustine says, things cannot give themselves their forms, because things cannot give powers which they do not have.

If human reason can trace how some forms exist as they do, why should it be impossible to alter these forms? Christians say god made the forms of the world to be as they are. But if we use reason, though surely of a less capable kind than god's, why could men not alter these forms? We make new forms of metals by mixing together existing ones in certain ways. This is the aim of alchemy, which has always had as its goal to create gold from base metals. This is discussed by your predecessor Michael Scot in a text called a *Curious Investigation Concerning the Nature of the* Sun *and Moon.*

Master Theodore: Does this make us god-like?

Frederick II: Only in the way that theologians and religious sages have always said, namely, that in having reason we are in the image of god.

Master Theodore: There has been no success in creating gold.

Frederick II: That is correct. Our knowledge about this seems quite limited at the present time, but I see no reason in principle why certain forms cannot be combined with others following careful processes to produce new forms. We know this from our ability to make better metal swords than the ancients possessed.

Ethics

Master Theodore: You are saying there are no limits in principle to reason's ability to know about the world and the processes by which it operates. Can knowledge also teach us how to live?

Frederick II: This was never said to be true in the scriptures themselves. The rules by which to live are given to the Jews in the Torah. These include the ten commandments but also the entirety of the Law.

Master Theodore: Christians accept the ten commandments, but see no reason to follow the rest of the detailed requirements of the Law.

Frederick II: That is so. For Christians the rules of the ten commandments, which are revealed by god himself, are a guide for how to live a good life. Maimonides says that these commands are not inconsistent with reason, but they are not known in their fullness and specificity by reason, but only by revelation. Most Christian thinkers follow this view, though some come close to suggesting that the ten commandments can be known by reason alone.

Master Theodore: Jesus seems not to refer to these commands but offers a simpler list of commands to guide our lives.

Frederick II: Jesus says that all the commands of god can be summarized simply: love god and love others as you love yourself. These simple rules are nowhere said to be known by reason, but rather because they are spoken by Jesus himself. Jesus does not urge his listeners to be guided by their reason, but rather by love. Christian ethics are based upon the duty to love, not to reason. Reason is of no particular use and can even be an impediment to living a moral life. Jesus speaks often of the need for a simple, child-like faith, as opposed to a process of reasoning in order to live a good life.

Master Theodore: God's commands are known then by revelation, either that of the Hebrew bible or better yet, by what Jesus himself teaches.

Frederick II: One cannot reason one's way to a love of god or one's fellow man. Love of god and one's fellow man is the result of a will turning toward god. As Paul says, the ability to love transcends the ability to reason. Love reaches beyond reason and teaches us what reason cannot teach: how to live well.

Master Theodore: This is the simple teaching of the ancient Christian scriptures. But it seems there have been other and newer thoughts about how to live since the days when scripture revealed god's will.

Frederick II: Yes, the first such thoughts have arisen from the institution of the church itself. The early church pointed Christians toward the love of god and neighbor. But now we have the colossus which is today's church, a hierarchical institution with many levels. At the top stands the pope. The church now defines what is ethical and what is not. It is the church which mediates between the simple commands of Jesus and the many beliefs and practices the church now says are necessary to live a life of faith. The teachings of the church do not contradict the commands of Jesus—at least for the most part—but they supplement them with many additional burdens.

Master Theodore: Is this similar to the Law of the Jews?

Frederick II: You could say this, but it is not quite the same. The Law is revealed in the Torah. The Law must be understood by learning form the Torah and its various authoritative interpretations. There is no overarching power among the Jews to say what must and what must not be believed Christian beliefs and practices today follow whatever the church requires—and this changes with the whims of the popes.

Master Theodore: Your acquaintance Francis of Assisi speaks to this.

Frederick II: Yes, he sought to return Christianity to a simpler form, unburdened by the extraneous requirements of today's worldly church. But the simplicity he preached is also based on love and not on reason.

Master Theodore: So reason plays little role in Christian ethics?

Frederick II: This has been true for Christianity since its earliest days. But today we are seeing for the first time a new teaching. Consider the teaching of Peter Abelard. Abelard says that philosophers teach ethics based upon our natural reason. He says that our reason takes us to what he calls a kind of "natural law," a law of ethics comparable to the regularity which many objects in the natural world display. For Abelard this natural law of ethics is the same as the commands of Jesus: to love god and one's neighbor. But what he says is very new. He says that we can learn these two commands through our natural reason alone, unaided by revelation.

Master Theodore: On what basis does he say this?

Frederick II: He commends the power of reason as taught by the ancient philosophers. He aims in this way to bring reason and Christian ethics much closer together. In this way he goes beyond what Maimonides says, that the commands of god are consistent with reason. Abelard says that these simple commands can be known by natural reason.

Master Theodore: This seems to be a very new view in recent years.

Frederick II: Yes. We see many of today's Christian philosophers and theologians attempting to bring reason and Christianity closer together.

We have discussed how this is so concerning the operation of secondary causes in the universe. Christian thinkers today assert that human reason can teach us these things without god's regular intervention. But Abelard goes further: he says that reason can teach us not only the operation of secondary causes, but the general principles of ethics as well. This extends the scope of reason far more widely. The attempt to bring together reason and revelation in Christian ethics is what these authors call "natural law."

Master Theodore: Abelard is not alone in this.

Frederick II: By no means. We see this in William of Auvergne, Robert Grosseteste and our own great Albert. I have spoken with Albert about these matters and urged him to follow natural reason as far as possible without relying on scripture.

Master Theodore: He has learned this well. He conducts many investigations into the operations of nature. He follows reason in all his experimental work. He gives reason its full due before turning to revelation.

Frederick II: He teaches this practice to his students as well, including our own Thomas of Aquino who has studied Aristotle at the university I founded in Naples.

Master Theodore: Do you think we can determine the rules of human behavior from natural reason alone?

Frederick II: We will discuss this further when we speak about government. Here I will say only this: much depends on whether we think god has placed within us not only the desire, but also the ability, to know both what is true and what is good.

ON ISLAM

Frederick II: Let us speak now about the most recent monotheistic faith, that of the Muslims.

Master Theodore: Is this a new faith or does it derive from Judaism and Christianity?

Frederick II: It is new but it also draws elements from these earlier faiths. Many of those who are called messengers, or prophets, in the Qur'an can be found in the earlier scriptures. At times the prophet Muhammad seems to suggest that his message and the messages of the earlier prophets—Noah, Abraham, Moses and Jesus, for example—are very similar, though given to different peoples in different languages.

Master Theodore: Is this the final monotheism we shall see, or are there perhaps more to come?

Frederick II: The Muslims say that Muhammad is the last and final prophet. There will be no more. The Qur'an never says this directly, though in one passage it refers to Muhammad as "the seal of the prophets" which is taken to mean that there will be no more. It seems from the Hadith that Muhammad thought of himself this way as well. Most Muslims, including even the thoughtful Averroes, say that because Islam is the most perfect religion, it must be the last. As a logician, however, Averroes surely knows better than to credit this argument. The Muslims cannot know Islam is the final religion, of course. The god of the Qur'an is perfectly free to will whatever he pleases, and if he wishes to send another prophet in the future who is to say that he cannot do this?

Master Theodore: Some people, especially your enemies in the church, say that you are a follower of this faith.

Frederick II: Yes, I have heard this. I grew up as a young boy among many Muslims and I am familiar with their beliefs and their customs. I speak fluently in Arabic, which is the language of the Qur'an, and I often correct the translations of my scholars. I admire their wisest philosophers and I respect their wisest rulers. In this way I was able to gain the liberation of the Christian holy sites by negotiating with, and not warring with al-Kamil.

Master Theodore: Your critics also point to your concubines and to your use of Saracens to protect you.

Frederick II: I have adopted the Arabic custom of numerous wives. This, by the way, was the practice of ancient Jewish rulers like Solomon, who is much admired by Jews and Christians alike. Solomon had many more wives than I. And it is true that I rely on Saracens for my personal protection. But this I do as a matter of expediency. In this way I know that my safety will not be compromised by agents of the pope. But I am not a member of the Muslim faith.

Master Theodore: This faith spread very rapidly from its earliest days.

Frederick II: Yes, Muhammad himself fought many battles to secure and to expand this faith. And his successors were able to conquer all of Arabia, the Near East, Persia, North Africa and even a large portion of Spain on the European continent. Many people have become Muslims by conviction, but almost always after having been conquered by Muslim armies.

Master Theodore: Let us discuss this faith.

The Qualities of God

Frederick II: We should begin with the qualities of god, or al-lah (the god) as is said in Arabic.

Master Theodore: How is the god of the Muslims to be understood?

Frederick II: Not much is said directly about this god in the Qur'an. The Qur'an speaks far more about god's commands for men than about god himself.

Master Theodore: Yet there are descriptions of god in the Qur'an.

Frederick II: Yes, all but one of the suras begins by affirming god's quality of mercy. They begin with the words "In the name of God, the Lord of Mercy, the giver of Mercy." It is not clear who is speaking here, whether the spirit Gabriel or Muhammad himself. But in many other places the Qur'an speaks of god's mercy.

Master Theodore: There are other qualities ascribed to god as well.

Frederick II: Yes, the Qur'an ascribes to god the seven perfections thought to characterize man. These are knowledge, life, power, will, vision, hearing and speech. Man is the most perfect creature in the creation, and is said to possess some degree of each of these perfections. God is said to possess all these qualities perfectly, in a fashion far beyond the way in which they are found in man.

Master Theodore: Does god have other qualities?

Frederick II: The spirit Gabriel also calls god the controller, the Holy One, the source of peace, the grantor of security, the guardian over all, the almighty, the compeller, the truly great, the creator, the originator and the shaper. These qualities all seem to me to be contained in the perfections of man which we mentioned. We might in this regard recall the words of Christian philosophers who say that out of respect we humans give all the best names to god, especially that he is "good."

Master Theodore: Can Muslims know these things for sure?

Frederick II: We shall have to look further at this, including the views of the Muslim philosophers who speak to this. For god is also said to be far beyond the ability of human beings to know him. It is said that god's knowledge and god's ways differ radically from those of men and that men cannot know god directly. The Qur'an itself says we can know god only by revelation, or behind a veil, or through a messenger. God speaks directly only occasionally in the Qur'an, and even there it is only what is reported by the spirit Gabriel. It seems that it was given only to Moses to speak directly with god, and even that through a veil.

Master Theodore: This seems to be the same difficulty experienced by all the monotheistic faiths: god must be thought of as immeasurably far from man, but also enough alike to be known in some way.

Frederick II: Yes, this is well said. A literal interpreter of the Qur'an raised this question in saying that "nothing in this world is analogous to the next one, except the names."

Master Theodore: Is the Qur'an then, as the word of god, a part of god from all time or did god create the Qur'an?

Frederick II: A very interesting question, Master Theodore. If the Qur'an was from the beginning a part of god—as god's word, so to say—this comes perilously close to polytheism. Muslims, for example, reject entirely the idea that Jesus was a part of god—as god's word—from the beginning. This, they say, is the teaching of polytheism to which they are unalterably opposed. God has no "partners." One and only one god exists, a god who is indivisible. Even god's traits or attributes, which we humans list separately, are one with god.

Master Theodore: Muslims regard Jesus as a prophet, but as no part of god himself.

Frederick II: Yes. Although Muslims share some beliefs in common with Christianity, they deny the central belief of Christianity. This is why it is very difficult to reconcile Christianity and Islam in a serious way. For Muslims god does not have two parts or two persons, leave aside three; god is one, purely and simply. For this reason many Muslim theology scholars, especially those known as Mutazilites, denied that the Qur'an is or ever was a part of god from the beginning. They believed that the Qur'an was created by god.

Master Theodore: It seems that god's revelations have taken place in time, some earlier to the Jews, some later to the Christians, and some finally to the Arabs. This suggests that the Qur'an was given within human time.

Frederick II: Yes, but you must recall what philosophers say, namely, that what occurs in time for humans is not experienced in this way by god. Averroes wisely says that philosophers should not teach the doctrine of a god outside of time to the mass of people, as they cannot comprehend it.

Master Theodore: As god's creation, which was intended to be understood by man, the Qur'an is then subject to interpretation.

Frederick II: This is much the same for the Hebrew scriptures and the

Christian gospel. That is why the Jews have the Mishnah, for example. The words of god may be sublimely true, but they are spoken to human beings who are limited and fallible. As we will discuss later, it is the role of prophets to receive the words of god and to present them in ways that the great mass of men can understand.

Master Theodore: But not all Muslim scholars believe that men are free to interpret the Qur'an.

Frederick II: This is true. But it is difficult to see how this view can be maintained. There is much in the Qur'an that is unclear and much which even seems self-contradictory. To say, as some such as Hanbal have said, do not interpret the Qur'an but just believe—this is an attractive view only to those who are not thoughtful or who see no role for reason in human affairs. Even the great and influential Muslim thinker al-Ghazali, who spoke forcefully about the limits of human reason, acknowledged there are places in the Qur'an that can be legitimately interpreted.

Master Theodore: How could it be otherwise?

Frederick II: To fail to interpret the Qur'an is simply to believe, perhaps rightly or wrongly, whatever one happens to understand are the commands of god. Who is to say then what is actually believed by people in these circumstances?

Master Theodore: Do the Muslim philosophers bring clarity to this?

Frederick II: The Muslim religious scholars—the mutakallimun—play the same role as the Jewish and Christian philosophers They aim to show that the teachings of Islam are consistent with reason, as far as reason can take them. They interpret the Qur'an in this way, trying to reconcile seeming contradictions and to explain matters which are in dispute. There are also, however, Muslim philosophers who are not theologians, which is different than Judaism or Christianity. The most important are Avicenna and Averroes, both of whom were at home as medical doctors, astronomers and jurists as well as commentators on philosophy and theology. They too think deeply about the claims of the Qur'an, but they do not do so as theologians but as philosophers.

Master Theodore: What do the Muslim philosophers teach about god and his qualities?

Frederick II: They teach that god is one, that he is simple and that he is incorporeal.

Master Theodore: This is consistent with Jewish and Christian philosophers.

Frederick II: There are of course differences, but what you say is mainly true.

Master Theodore: How do the philosophers know these are the qualities of god?

Frederick II: They demonstrate this through the use of reason. Avicenna, for example, teaches that unaided reason can demonstrate that god exists, is simple, is ineffable, is intelligent and is good. He offers what he believes are demonstrative proofs of this. Averroes, on the other hand, argues that reason cannot establish a demonstrative proof of the existence of god. He says that the only valid proofs of god's existence come from arguments from providence and invention. These are not deduced demonstrably but rather learned from observation, which is a kind of reason, though without absolute certainty.

Master Theodore: Do these teachings conflict with the Qur'an?

Frederick II: Their authors say they do not. If reason seems to contradict the Qur'an, one must look deeper. But for philosophers this does not mean that philosophy is in error, but that the words of the Qur'an are not properly understood. They say in such cases the words of the Qur'an must be understood allegorically. They must be interpreted as figures, written to bring the truth to the great mass of men, but also giving signs to the philosophers of the deeper meaning of the words.

Master Theodore: Do Avicenna and Averroes see this in the same way?

Frederick II: Yes, though Averroes is the deeper of the two. He says that the religious scholars do not offer genuine proofs of the existence of god or of other deep questions like the nature of the afterlife. He says that in this way many of the interpretations of the religious scholars lead the mass of men to unbelief and heresy. He says the mass of men should read the Qur'an just as it is written, with no interpretation. He says that the true demonstrative proofs of his own should not be shared with the masses and hence he only hints at them so that true philosophers can understand what he is saying. But all Muslim philosophers say they offer the same truths as the Qur'an, though in different words.

Master Theodore: This seems to make philosophy the arbiter of the Qur'an.

Frederick II: A very wise observation, Master Theodore, and one which philosophers aim to disguise as well as they can. So far as reason and faith travel together, reason is the arbiter of truth. What prophets reveal which goes beyond reason we will speak of shortly.

Master Theodore: You have caused Averroes' work to be translated into Hebrew and Latin.

Frederick II: Yes, so that we in the west might have the benefit of his thought. Averroes is not much followed in Muslim circles, though he is the best of the Muslim philosophers.

Master Theodore: Why do you favor Averroes?

Frederick II: Averroes is a better interpreter of Aristotle than Avicenna. His commentaries are invaluable guides to understanding the texts of Aristotle; Avicenna often—perhaps intentionally—mixes up what is from Aristotle and what is from other philosophers like Plotinus.

Master Theodore: Both Muslim religious scholars and Avicenna teach that the world was created by god, who is the first cause of everything. More thoughtful philosophers say that it cannot be proven whether the world was created or is eternal. Averroes, following Aristotle, says there can be no demonstrative proof the world was created and not eternal. As we have said, Maimonides follows him in this. This hints at serious questions about Averroes' own proofs of creation from the arguments for providence and invention.

Master Theodore: The question of whether the world is created by god or is eternal turns out to be very significant.

Frederick II: Yes, much follows from this. This is perhaps surprising, as it might seem that this question—about which very little can be known in any event—would be found only in the province of random and useless speculations.

Master Theodore: The Muslim debate about this has been very significant for Jewish and Christian thought as well.

Frederick II: Yes, all faiths have had to come to terms with Aristotle. As we have said, Aristotle searches for a first cause of motion, not of being which he says is eternal. Muslim philosophers say that god is not simply the first cause of motion but of being itself. As we have discussed, both Jewish and Christian thinkers agree with Muslim philosophers in this. Muslim philosophers have helped to refine for their Jewish and Christian followers the language that god is the cause of all being, the first cause of the world.

Master Theodore: Were Muslim philosophers the first to argue such things?

Frederick II: No, some of them learned in turn from the earlier Christian thinker John Philoponus, who addressed arguments against Aristotle concerning the eternity of the world. But Muslim philosophers offer a comprehensive argument and an attractive language in which to describe god: they say that god's essence guarantees his existence and that god is for this reason a necessary being. Christian philosophers have found this useful and compelling and it is widely taught in Christian circles as well.

Master Theodore: Muslim philosophers also say that god's existence can be known, as least to a certain extent, by the world which he has created.

Frederick II: On this point they are in agreement with the words of the Qur'an. The Qur'an says "In the succession of night and day, and in what God created in the heavens and earth, these truly are signs for those who are aware of Him." These signs can be read by the natural reason of men, and are so obvious that only the willfully ignorant turn away from them,

Master Theodore: This view is also held by the Jews and the Christians.

Frederick II: Yes, they argue that the order of the world demonstrates the existence and nature of god who created it. All these accounts which speak of the order of the world, and the way in which it is designed to benefit the ends of human beings, however, must eventually attempt to explain the disorder and sinfulness which is in the world. We will talk of this later.

Master Theodore: We have so far spoken of what man can know of god. What do the philosophers say that god knows, and how does he know it?

Frederick II: This is a question which must be addressed by all faiths which seek to reconcile themselves with philosophy. Following Plato, if knowledge is that which knows what is truly real and never changes, can god have knowledge of the created world which is always changing? Can there be true knowledge, even for god, of particulars? How is this possible if god's knowledge is never-changing? Some Islamic philosophers say that god can have knowledge of particulars, as one might expect.

Master Theodore: What do they say?

Frederick II: Some say that god knows particulars, which come and go, in a universal way. This seems to me meaningless. Others say that god knows unchanging universals but also knows particulars in a different manner. They say that humans know particulars as a result of their causes but god knows them as the one who has established these causes. This too seems to me to say very little that can be comprehended. Others say that god of course knows all things, but the manner of his knowing is so distant from human knowing that humans cannot fathom the ways of god's knowledge. This seems to me comprehensible but not very helpful as an explanation.

Master Theodore: Averroes speaks to this question.

Frederick II: Yes, he criticizes his predecessors for saying that god's knowledge is unchanging. He says that knowing something before it exists and knowing it when it does exist must necessarily be two different kinds of knowledge. He says it is difficult to conceive how god could have knowledge of particulars which come and go. Knowledge of what is possible is different than knowledge of what exists. He says that god's knowledge, if that is the correct word, is very different from human knowledge.

Master Theodore: What then is the warrant for calling both by the name of "knowledge?"

Frederick II: Here we return again to the question that has confronted Christians as well. As we have discussed, at the Lateran Council in 1215 Christian theologians said that god's powers are far different and superior to ours, but bear sufficient likeness to ours to warrant the same name. This is true for Muslims as well. If there were no similarity between god and man, what is it exactly that man would worship but perhaps an empty X?

Master Theodore: If god were to be conceived as being reason itself, necessarily, this could mean that man's reason is at least a pale image of god's.

Frederick II: Yes, this is the Christian doctrine since the gospel of John. God is the logos, or reason, and man partakes in that. Human reason, then, is an illumination from god. This is also the view of some Muslim theologians and philosophers. But over the past several centuries the Muslim faith has moved very far away from this view. The ascendant view—Averroes refers to the Asharites as those who constitute orthodox Muslims in this age—is not that god is reason and necessarily so, but that god possesses reason as an attribute which he can employ as he wishes. They say that if reason were a necessary aspect of god's being, it would act as a limit to god's freedom to will as he wishes. Reason, they say, would cause god to have to act in certain ways, and this would stand as a limit to the free and unbounded will of god.

Master Theodore: God, then, would not be necessarily just, as the Mutazilites say,

Frederick II: Upon this view god is not bound by anything at all, and is not constrained by human ideas of what is reason or justice or any other virtue. God is pure unbounded will.

God's Will

Master Theodore: Let us speak more of god's unfettered will.

Frederick II: As we have said, god's will is of course important to each of the three monotheistic faiths. For the Jews it is god's will through which he displays his power and his protection of his chosen people. For Christians god's will is even more important; it is through god's will that whatever befalls each and every human being in the world occurs. This may be implied in Judaism but it is more clearly said in Christianity. But it is in Islam that god's will takes on its greatest importance.

Master Theodore: One sees this clearly in the Qur'an.

Frederick II: Yes, it is very pronounced there. But one also finds this not only among Muslim theological scholars but among philosophers as well. Al-farabi, for example, speaks often of god's unfettered will.

Master Theodore: Why is god's will so important in Islam?

Frederick II: We have spoken of god's attributes. The Qur'an says that god sees and hears all. But philosophers say that god's seeing and hearing cannot be the same as human seeing and hearing; god has no eyes and no ears. The Qur'an is silent about matters like these. The most important point is that people believe they are being watched and heard; in what mode this occurs is not important. So too with god's speech. God does not speak like humans, for he has no tongue; what is important is that people believe that god can and does communicate his will, though perhaps in his own way.

Master Theodore: This is true of god's knowledge as well.

Frederick II: Yes, as we have discussed it is not possible to comprehend the mode of god's knowing, only to believe that god knows everything. Philosophers say that god's knowledge is very different than human knowledge.

Master Theodore: What is the meaning of these views?

Frederick II: It means that each of the human qualities we assign to god cannot be known directly but only on analogy with human qualities. We can give up all of the conventional notions of god—his corporality, his speech, his hearing and vision, and his intelligence—and still worship a god that possesses these qualities, even if we do not know how.

Master Theodore: Is this true of god's will as well?

Frederick II: Most Muslim believers understand god's will as a more expansive form of human will. The always thoughtful Averroes, however, says "there is no counterpart to [god's] will in the empirical world" and "the quality of [god's] will cannot be conceived." But he understood that the idea of god's will is indispensable to Islam. If god had no will—and human beings know what it is to will—what is the point of obedience to god? It is through his will that god rewards and punishes, and this is the core of Muslim belief. If god has no will, there is no meaning to Islam.

Master Theodore: God's will, then, is like human will but far more powerful and expansive.

Frederick II: Yes, this is so. We have spoken already of what is called negative theology, in which we think away the figures of human qualities in order to go closer to a true idea of god. We can say that god is not corporeal, that god does not think and speak and see and hear like we do. Negative theology can multiply its "nots." It also says that god cannot be captured by not-nots. For example, we say that warmth is not heavy. But warmth is also not-not heavy. God is beyond the distinctions of not and not-not; he transcends all such distinctions. The only human quality that a Muslim's god cannot do without is will; this is the inescapable human attribute necessary to understand and to worship god. We know what will is. God may have it in greater abundance, but not in a way that passes human understanding. No will, no god.

Master Theodore: How does god will?

Frederick II: The Qur'an speaks often about this. It says that god wills freely. God may will whatever he pleases. The Qur'an, quoting god directly it seems, says: "When We will something to happen, all that We say is 'Be,' and it is." God seems to speak things into existence, but it is not the mode of his willing that is important; it is the fact that god wills. The Qur'an says that humans do not comprehend anything about god's knowledge "except what He wills." However god may speak, it is as an expression of his will that humans understand it.

Master Theodore: Are there any bounds to god's will?

Frederick II: God can create whenever, wherever and whatever he pleases. God created the entirety of the earth and the seven heavens above. The Qur'an says this was easy for god.

Master Theodore: God could create the world all over again?

Frederick II: Yes, god can and indeed will make a second creation, one in which believers will be rewarded and sinners punished. This is the day of reckoning when humans will come back to life to live according to their earthly choices. The Qur'an says that because god created a first creation, he will create a second one. This of course does not follow logically, but it points to god's unbounded will.

Master Theodore: The sheer willfulness of Islam's god seems far more pronounced that that of the Jewish or Christian god.

Frederick II: Yes, it is often said the principal quality of Islam's god is that of mercy. But god's mercy seems to operate in a limited way. God creates the world for men, which is surely an act of mercy, he sends "signs" to men, and he welcomes back those who have erred and who return to the correct path. Those who do not return to the correct path, however—those who remain in disbelief— god treats with no mercy at all. They are condemned to the perpetual fires of hell. But in either case—whether god chooses to offer mercy or not—he does so as an act of his will. God's will lies behind and is expressed through all of his acts, including whatever mercy he may choose to extend to individuals.

Master Theodore: Does god will necessarily or freely? Could god will differently than he has?

Frederick II: The best Muslim philosophers say that god wills necessarily. God surely does not do what he does for no reason at all. How could this be true? Both Avicenna and Averroes say that god wills necessarily. To explain how god can have a permanent underlying eternal will, and still be able to will particulars to come and go out of existence, Averroes inserts the idea of "action" into the process. An eternal will, he says, could not create a world in time unless god's will "acts" from time to time. This seems to me not very helpful as a resolution of this problem. But both philosophers say that god wills as he must or god would suffer the imperfection of randomness.

Mater Theodore: But their views are not very influential with most Muslims.

Frederick II: The great preponderance of Muslim theologians believe there is nothing necessary about god's will. Such necessity would be a boundary to god's free willing, and as such cannot be. Averroes is not much known or followed among Muslim theologians. It is my intention that he become better known among Christians and Jews, as he deserves to be.

Master Theodore: If god wills freely, with no bounds to his will, this raises several questions. The first is, if god can and does will freely, why did he will to create the world and its heavens?

Frederick II: An excellent question, Master Theodore. The world and its seven heavens are a very complex creation. Why did god choose to create this? The Qur'an says many times that there was a purpose behind god's creation of the world. But what is that purpose? The Qur'an never speaks to this, which is wise, because it is not a subject about which anything could be known. About what god might have done, but has not, there is only unfounded speculation.

Master Theodore: Did god create the world so that human beings might worship him, and to judge those who do and who do not?

Frederick II: The Qur'an often gives this impression, but that cannot be true. A completely self-sufficient, omnipotent god has no need to create human beings to worship him. What could the worship of so lowly a creature as man mean to god? The Qur'an says that "God does not need his creatures." God does not need anything from man or any other creature; this would suggest a need, or a limitation, or an imperfection of god, which cannot be. As has been said, human beings need to worship god for their own sakes, not because god needs it.

Master Theodore: Why then would god create the world?

Frederick II: The Qur'an never answers this question, which it would no doubt consider an impertinence. The Qur'an says only that god did not create the world for his own amusement, which he could have found within himself. The Qur'an is very repetitive and says many times that god had a purpose in creating the world—but does not say what is that purpose.

Master Theodore: What do the philosophers say about this?

Frederick II: Avicenna speaks plainly about this, and in a way that seems to contradict the Qur'an. He says that not only did god have no purpose in creating the world, but that god could not have had a purpose. For god to have a goal or a purpose in creating the world implies that god has desires, and desires imply a lack or a need. God could have no such lack or need.

Master Theodore: If god had no need to create the world why did he do so?

Frederick II: This is a difficult question for all three of the monotheistic faiths, and for any faith for that matter. God might be said to have created the world, and humans within it, because he loves his creation. But again, love implies need and this cannot be so. Perhaps Plato has come closest to offering an answer to such a question. He says that a god created the world out of an overflowing and boundless generosity. This suggests, however, that the world is a kind of emanation from god, which is very far from the view of creation in the three monotheistic faiths about which we have been speaking.

Master Theodore: Perhaps this question cannot be answered. But there is another question as well. Let us grant that for whatever reason, god chose to create the world. If god is free to create as he will, why did he create this world in just the way it exists? Why not a different world?

Frederick II: The Qur'an never addresses this question either. Philosophers who say that god's creative acts are necessary say that god had no choice but to create just this world.

Master Theodore: This may be true but it does not say very much about why this world and not another.

Frederick II: A fair point, Master Theodore. Philosophers actually say a bit more, as they must. If this world is necessary, and if god is both good and merciful, this must be the best of all possible created worlds. How could it be otherwise?

Master Theodore: This must follow. The created world must be good. The Qur'an describes many ways in which this is so, many ways in which the created world is well-suited to human beings. But there is also evil in this world. Is it not therefore true that the best possible world must be a world in which there is evil? Could not god have created a world in which there is no evil?

Frederick II: We will speak of that soon enough. Let me say here only that in Islam we know that god wills, but we do not know why god wills just as he does. It is not for human beings to second guess god.

Master Theodore: There is one remaining question, which is even more perplexing. Let us set aside the question of whether god had a purpose in creating the world. Does god himself have a purpose?

Frederick II: God is said to be an eternal, uncreated being. There was not a time before god was. As we have discussed, what is eternal and uncreated cannot be said to have a purpose. Only what is created can have a purpose. Creation suggests an end, a goal, a purpose. One can ask a sculptor, for example, why he creates a sculpture. The sculptor might say in order to honor someone, or to serve as a gift, or to receive a fee, or to create beauty which did not previously exist. One can always seek the purpose of what is created.

Master Theodore: But god is said to be uncreated.

Frederick II: Yes, god is said to be eternal. What is eternal cannot be said to have a purpose. Aristotle said that the world is eternal and therefore it can have no purpose. Its parts may have a purpose, but the whole cannot. If we include god within all that is in being, and if god is eternal, then god and by implication the world, cannot be said to have a purpose.

Master Theodore: Perhaps god created himself.

Frederick II: None of the three monotheistic faiths holds that god was created, even by himself. God is eternal, unchanging and uncreated. When one looks at the world of all that is in being, including god, and asks why this rather than nothing exists, there is no good answer. Such a world with its god could not be said to have any purpose. The most one can say is that god simply is, and that he chose to create the world, though we do not know why.

Master Theodore: Considering an eternal world of being, or a world created by an eternal god, comes finally to the same point. The entire created world can have a purpose, but the whole world of being including god, does not.

Frederick II: The purpose of all being, including god and his creation, can have no purpose. In this way atomistic determinism and a world created by an eternal god come very much to the same end. Human beings can be said to have a purpose in a god-created world; the Qur'an speaks of human life as a diversion and a testing for eternal life of god's blessing or condemnation. But why such a god should exist cannot be said.

The Created World

Master Theodore: What is the world of a freely creating god like? Some say that god creates the world and then leaves it to run itself, except for occasional miraculous interventions.

Frederick II: This is very far from the view of Muslims. There are, as we shall discuss, several Muslim philosophers who come close to this view, but the dominant Muslim view—of ordinary Muslims and Muslim religious scholars alike—is very far from this. The Asharite view, which Averroes calls orthodoxy, understands god to be very deeply involved in the day-to-day operations of the world.

Master Theodore: God not only creates the world, but he sustains it. Some say that such a god sustains the world by leaving it to run itself, except for occasional miraculous interventions.

Frederick II: Jews and Christians also believe that god sustains the world he has created. This is held as it must be, because to deny it would suggest that god no longer cares about the world he created. Both believe that god can still intervene in the world, but there have been very few known instances of god's intervention in the world of the Jews and the Christians in the past millennium. Jews and Christians often ask what this means—where is god?—and while they assume that god can intervene if he wishes to, the notion of god's regular intervention plays a tangential role in these faiths. It is found in prayer and in the miracles attributed to saints, but it is unclear to what extent, if any, god answers prayers.

Master Theodore: It is very different with Islam.

Frederick II: Islam's god is always present in sustaining his creation, and therefore every historical act is looked at as a sign from god. Consider this. The Christian god is said to be aware of the fall of every sparrow. But the Qur'an says that god holds up the birds of the air.

This god not only knows all that happens, he makes to occur each and every specific event which occurs. Islam's god is continually present, holding up the world, as it were. Without god's continuing will to sustain the world at every moment, the world would end immediately. God continually wills the existence and order of his creation; without this will the world would cease to exist. Each and every being in the created world depends from moment to moment on god's will.

Master Theodore: This raise questions about the role of cause and effect in the world. God is a necessary being, whose essence guarantees his existence. He is the cause of all else; god is the primary cause of everything.

Frederick II: Yes, this much is held by Jews, Muslims and Christians alike. But how then does god choose to order the world he has created? In what way, if at all, does he employ secondary causes? Here there is a vast difference between Judaism and Christianity and the orthodox Muslim view.

Master Theodore: God could order the world by giving secondary causes their own power. This would be a power derived from god, but held by natures in the world god has created.

Frederick II: Yes, for Avicenna and even more so for Averroes this is true. But the orthodox Muslim view is very different. In this view god shares none of his power with any created being. God creates many beings with what could be called their "natures" but these natures have no power of their own. No nature of any created being proceeds out of itself. No natures have an intrinsic power to act in their own right or to create or shape the nature of other created beings. This, which is believed by all orthodox Muslims, is said most clearly by al- Ghazali.

Master Theodore: This suggests there are no genuine secondary causes.

Frederick II: This is correct. And more than that, it raises the question whether any of god's creations actually have their own "natures." God is the agent of everything, first and second causes alike. God is the direct agent of a fire's burning. God is not the indirect agent, who in his wisdom gave to fire its own potency to burn. God intervenes as agent each and every time fire burns. If god wished fire not to burn in a specific instance, it would not. If god wished to give fire's potency to burn to another part of creation, say a stone, he could do that. God is the direct agent of each and every occurrence in the world.

Master Theodore: This suggests why Muslims read each and every occurrence carefully, for acts within the world are not distant from god but are caused by him. That is why Muhammad sees victory or defeat in every battle as a sign from god.

Frederick II: Yes, and what is true of battles and other important events is also true of each action in the world, no matter how small and insignificant. What looks as if a fire causes itself to burn when the conditions are correct, is the act of god. One might say that what you and I regard as causality looks to Muslim orthodoxy as simultaneity. All causality lies with god. Fire's burning is due to no quality of fire, but to god's direct will. This is to deny to the things of the world any "nature" at all.

Master Theodore: Each and every time?

Frederick II: Each and every time.

Master Theodore: Yet the Qur'an also says that human beings will find no change in god's practices.

Frederick II: That is correct. This regularity, however, is not credited to causes or powers lying within created entities, but is called a "habit of god."

Master Theodore: All regularity in the created world then is contingent on god's ever-present will.

Frederick II: Yes, the entire world is contingent not simply as a general premise, but in each and every aspect of its existence. The world can change in wholly unpredictable ways, if god wills it to be so.

Master Theodore: Do all Muslim philosophers follow this view?

Frederick II: No, Averroes for example, does not. Averroes says this view is self-contradictory. He asks if the entire created world is wholly contingent at every given moment, where is the order in the world? Such a view, he says, condemns the created world to an essentially random and chaotic state, with no possible knowledge of cause and effect. If the world is essentially random and chaotic, it is not permitted to human beings to know anything at all about this world. With no order in the world, however, how then can we know of god as the creator of this world? Without the assumption of causality, it is impossible to know anything about the world and its creator. Without order which we can understand, how can we infer a creator, much less one that is merciful? A world governed by what looks to human beings only as chance makes god's existence doubtful as well.

Master Theodore: This would be very much like the world of the atomists.

Frederick II: Yes. Averroes asks: if there were no order in the world, how could a miracle be possible? Miracles are said to be the direct intervention of god in the world, but how would we know they were miracles unless set against the regular working of cause and effect?

Master Theodore: What do orthodox Muslims say about this?

Frederick II: Al-Ghazali says that all that we call nature is miraculous, and all miracles are in this sense natural, that is, created by god.

Master Theodore: How does Averroes respond?

Frederick II: He says that this view denies all natural human knowledge of the world. Nothing could then be known. And the claim of an entirely contingent world made by al-Ghazali and others would be unable to be known as well. He says this view is self-contradictory.

Master Theodore: Does al-Ghazali deny the possibility of all human knowledge?

Frederick II: Al-Ghazali says that logic and mathematics are permissible areas of human investigation. They are abstract and concern the relation of ideas to one another. They do not speak to the question of existing beings such as god and the world. About the beings in the world all that can be said is that they are always contingent upon god's ever-present will.

Master Theodore: What does Averroes say?

Frederick II: Averroes argues that if created beings do not have natures which are fixed by god, there is nothing that can be known about them. But we do have such knowledge. If we do not think that what god has created is reasonable, and is therefore unable to be known, how is knowledge of god in any way possible? Averroes argues that it is permissible to be skeptical about the extent of human reason, but to deny reasoning about the created world entirely, undermines the ground of this skepticism. Al-Ghazali says the proper purpose of reason is to turn upon itself and demonstrate how little it knows about the created world.

Master Theodore: It seems that the utter contingency of the created world reaches very deeply into the Muslim faith. Why did the Asharites stake out such an extreme position regarding the impotence of human reason?

Frederick II: The impotence of human reason is a direct consequence of the belief in the impotence of natural things in the created world. Aristotle asserted that the natural world—though uncreated—is not impotent. Entities in this world have natures and these natures can be known. So also these natures have the capability to affect other entities and the ways in which they do so can be known as well. This, I think, is the correct, and I would say normal view. It was not sufficient for the Asharites that god's will should create the world and remain only in principle able to affect it going forward. For them god's will is not only superior to all other wills, but is the only will, the only agency there is. To impute to any created being any degree of its own free will, agency or cause is an affront to the magnificence of god.

Master Theodore: God's will must be not only the most powerful will, but the only genuine will.

Frederick II: Yes.

Master Theodore: Do you agree with Averroes' criticism of this view?

Frederick II: Yes, it seems to me we do have the possibility of genuine knowledge of the created world. Averroes says "true knowledge is knowledge of the thing according to what it is in itself." This is the view which I expressed in my book on hunting with falcons.

Master Theodore: The Asharites deny human reason because they deny that god must act with reason. They deny reason as an essential attribute of god in order to remove all bounds from god. God wills as he whims, and there is no reason for what god does.

Frederick II: The Asharites have secured god's omnipotence at the cost of his reason and also, as we shall see, of his goodness.

Ethics

Master Theodore: We have spoken of the limits of reason in a world created by a freely willing god. What can we know about how to live in such a world, that is, what we usually call by the name of ethics?

Frederick II: Some Muslim theologians have said that man can have knowledge of good and evil. The Mutazilites argued that it is possible for unaided human reason to know something about what is good and evil. They said particularly that men can know that some actions are just or unjust. They said that such knowledge, of course, could not conflict with what is revealed in the Qur'an. What is revealed takes us further than natural reason, but god would not reveal anything which is not in accord with human reason.

Master Theodore: They say too that man can not only know what is just and unjust, but is free to choose among these alternatives.

Frederick II: Yes, they say that in this way men will merit whatever blessedness or punishment awaits them. They argue that it would be unjust, and contrary to reason, for god to punish sinners if they do not sin of their own volition. The Qur'an says god "created death and life to test you and reveal which of you does best." What kind of test would it be if man had no ability to choose?

Master Theodore: This is not the orthodox opinion, however.

Frederick II: No, the orthodox opinion today is very different. The orthodox say that no man can know by natural reason what is just and unjust, what is good and what is evil. Only through what is revealed in the Qur'an can men know what is just and unjust, good and evil. Indeed, Orthodox believers go further. They say that nothing is just or unjust in itself. What god wills is what is just. And god may to choose to will as he pleases, willing sometimes one way and sometimes another. God does not act according to a higher or an intrinsic standard of justice or good. That would be to put the standard above god.

Master Theodore: This is to say that god is bound by neither an intrinsic standard nor a human standard of what is just.

Frederick II: This is exactly so. God is certainly not bound by human notions of justice or goodness. God does not will what is good or just; what god wills is good and just. This we must learn from the Qur'an and not from natural reason.

Master Theodore: Let us say then that god's will reveals what is just. Do men have the capacity to choose to do, or to fail to do, what god wills is just?

Frederick II: There are many passages in the Qur'an that offer support for the view of the Mutazilites. Why else would the Qur'an take as its main purpose to set out the straight path and to warn sinners to amend their ways and follow this path? What sense would this preaching and these exhortations make if men were not free to act? The whole of the Qur'an is an appeal, or perhaps better said a demand, to awaken and turn toward the correct path. This is not only the message of Muhammad, but also that of all the messengers who preceded Muhammad.

Master Theodore: The orthodox deny this.

Frederick II: Yes, the orthodox view is grounded in the omnipotence of god. Nothing happens save that god wills it. To grant men the ability to will freely, that is, to be agents is a reproach to the omnipotence of god. Though men are most alike to god in having wills, and not reason, their wills cannot be free. This would make men close to god, which is not possible. God is the agent who works though what are called human wills, but it is only the illusion of freedom which accompanies them. God is the agent and humans are deluded by the illusion they are acting freely.

Master Theodore: The Qur'an speaks often in this way, providing support for the orthodox view.

Frederick II: The Qur'an says that god leads some to stray and others not to stray. It says that it is god that causes men to be deceived, though it is not clear why god would choose to do this. It says that god could make everyone a believer if he willed it to be so. It is not at all clear why he does not do so, unless it is to test men. But then the Qur'an says that "no soul can believe except by God's will."

Master Theodore: This seems to deny man's free will entirely.

Frederick II: The Qur'an says straightforwardly that men do not have free will, but are guided by god. If men had free will, they would be like god. They would be agents who could out of themselves will things to be different, including their own choices. But since he is omnipotent, only god has this kind of agency. Man might be like god in that he has a will, but not in that his will is free. God controls everything.

Master Theodore: If god wishes to save someone, he wills that to happen. This seems like the Christian idea of grace.

Frederick II: Exactly. The Qur'an says that "God chooses for his Grace whom he will." And al-Ghazali speaks of god giving grace to men to repent.

Master Theodore: Are the Muslims better able to resolve the contradiction between god's omnipotence and man's free will than the Christian theologians?

Frederick II: To the contrary. The far greater stress on god's omnipotence in Islam simply makes the contradiction all the more visible. The more omnipotent is god, the less free are men's wills.

Master Theodore: Do the Muslim philosophers address this matter?

Frederick II: Averroes speaks to this. He says there are obvious self-contradictions in the Qur'an. God cannot be omnipotent as the only agency in the world, and humans free to choose as well. Moreover, why would god choose to punish people if their actions were not freely willed?

Master Theodore: How does Averroes address this?

Frederick II: He says where there are seeming contradictions in the Qur'an, human reason can offer interpretations of the Qur'an to resolve these contradictions. He himself offers what he says is a proof of how god's omnipotence and man's free will can be reconciled. What he chooses to resolve, however, is the consistency of god's foreknowledge and man's free will. He reconciles god's omniscience, but not his omnipotence, with man's free will. This is an easier task. I have never seen a satisfactory resolution of god's omnipotence with man's free will.

Master Theodore: It seems then that Islam, like Judaism or Christianity, argues that man cannot know with natural reason what is good and evil.

Frederick II: For this kind of knowledge revelation is needed. Why would revelation be useful, much less necessary, for men if they could know what is good and evil, what is just and unjust, with their natural reason? We cannot reason our way to knowledge of good and evil. This would truly make men god-like. We must rely on revelation to teach us what is good and evil.

Revelation, Prophets and the Law

Master Theodore: Let us discuss the role of revelation in Islam.

Frederick II: As you recall, the Qur'an says there are "signs" which god provides to teach men of his existence. These signs are said to be blessings from god, signs of his mercy. They can be seen and known by all men, presumably with natural reason alone.

Master Theodore: How far do these signs take men to knowledge about god? How much do they tell us about god?

Frederick II: They seem only to point to the existence of god, but no further with any certainty. That god favors order and that he is merciful must be inferred from these signs. They are said to display god's care for the world because the world is so well-ordered for human life.

Master Theodore: It is only through revelation that more about god, and everything about his commands is learned.

Frederick II: Yes, what is revealed by god to the prophets takes us beyond what natural reason can teach us. Revelation teaches us something about the qualities of god, but also what practices we are to follow to live a life in accord with god's will.

Master Theodore: How do these revelations appear?

Frederick II: They appear only to true prophets and even then often in a way that is shrouded. They are said to be the words of god, but each and every word is not clear to men. Without interpretation they do not answer all questions concerning their meaning. For example, as Averroes notes, the Qur'an does not tell us whether god is corporeal. Philosophers say that god cannot be corporeal but the words of the

Qur'an do not speak about this. The Qur'an leaves it open to the mass of men to carry images of god's corporeality in order to make it easier for them to believe. Philosophers know better.

Master Theodore: Revelation tells us what are god's commands, which cannot be known by natural reason.

Frederick II: Yes, even if revelation does not answer all questions fully, the words which are revealed take us far beyond reason.

Master Theodore: To whom are these revelations of god given?

Frederick II: Those who receive revelations from god are called prophets. The Qur'an says that "God chooses as his messengers or prophets whoever He wills." There is no known path to becoming a prophet; this is not a role to which humans can aspire either by merit or by training. God chooses his prophets.

Master Theodore: What are the qualities of true prophets?

Frederick II: Prophets are said to be wise. They know what philosophers know, but they do not know these things from training, but as a gift. Averroes says that prophets do not surpass the knowledge of philosophers but prophets have additional qualities which philosophers do not have.

Master Theodore: What are these additional qualities?

Frederick II: Prophets have an ability which philosophers lack. They have the ability to reveal the messages of god in images which common people can understand and which can move the mass of men in a way which the demonstrative knowledge of philosophers cannot. Philosophers often speak of three types of understanding: demonstrative, or certain knowledge; dialectical, or argumentative knowledge; and rhetoric, or the image of knowledge. The prophet combines these types of knowledge and is able to speak to the mass of men in images but also to guide the understanding of philosophers. Prophets possess fully actualized minds.

Master Theodore: Are all true prophets then alike? Do they reveal the same god and the same commands of god?

Frederick II: The Qur'an says that all true prophets speak of the one and same god. Their words, however, differ. God sends prophets to different peoples and these prophets speak in different words and different languages. The Qur'an, for example, speaks of Noah, Abraham, Moses and Jesus, to name several prophets. Each of these prophets, though different in many ways, pointed to the one god which exists. They all warned of the error of their peoples' ways. They all warned above all of the two most serious sins of men: polytheism and worship of the things of this world.

Master Theodore: Jesus was like the other prophets in this regard?

Frederick II: Yes, he pointed to the one god whose messenger he was. His followers misunderstood his message, however, and thought of Jesus as part of god himself.

Master Theodore: Are some true prophets better than others?

Frederick II: Islam teaches that Muhammad is the best of the prophets. His revelations from god are clearer and more complete than those of other prophets.

Master Theodore: Many people claim to be prophets. How are we to know who is a genuine prophet and who is a false prophet?

Frederick II: As we have discussed, this is a difficult question, which permits of only imperfect answers. The Qur'an speaks of the "signs" of true prophets.

Master Theodore: What are these signs?

Frederick II: One sign is that true prophets often do miracles. Another is that they display genuine care for the people to whom they preach. Another is that they make predictions which come to pass. Noah, for example, preached against the sinfulness of his people and warned that they would be destroyed. Moses, for example, warned the Egyptian pharaoh against continuing to enslave his people and predicted destruction if they did not change their ways. There are many such instances in the Qur'an of god's destruction of peoples who did not follow the true path.

Master Theodore: But as we have discussed, men often do not see the consequences of their behavior until it is too late. How can this help determine a true from a false prophet until men learn afterward what comes to pass?

Frederick II: This is a fair question. The always thoughtful Averroes says that incidental effects like miracles and other signs are not dispositive. He says that the nature of the revelation itself is more important in determining a true prophet. This, however, as Averroes well knows is a very different answer and one which is dependent on understanding the true intent of a prophecy.

Master Theodore: Why can't god be clearer as to who are true prophets? After all, the Qur'an says that people seek more clarity. People would prefer the greater certainty of angels, rather than human prophets, to guide them. Muhammad had this advantage—he was spoken to by an angel.

Frederick II: The Qur'an says that of course god could send clearer, even unmistakable signs if he wished to do so. He could cause all people to believe if he wished to do so. It is only to say that this is apparently not god's will. The Qur'an says that the signs which god gives to his messengers are sufficient. In this way he tests human beings and metes out eternal punishment in hell to those who do not believe the signs.

Master Theodore: It seems then that Muslims must trust Muhammad in the first instance more than god.

Frederick II: This is true for Judaism, Christianity and Islam. Each faith must choose which messenger or messengers to trust when it comes to god's revelations.

Master Theodore: This choice has many consequences.

Frederick II: This is especially true in Judaism and Islam. Their prophets—Moses and Muhammad—do not simply preach the worship of the one true god. They also expound an entire way of life, including one which is conducive to the proper form of worship. This is what is called the Law.

Master Theodore: There is no comparable law for the Christians.

Frederick II: That is correct. Jesus spoke only of the need to love god and to love one's neighbors. The Jewish and Muslim prophets present a way of life which is to govern all aspects of peoples' behavior, including the proper way in which to worship god. In the case of Islam, some of these practices, rules and rituals are found in the Qur'an but many are found in the Hadith, which is an account of the life and acts of Muhammad.

Master Theodore: We have spoken of the recent development among some Christian philosophers of a "natural law." Is this true of Judaism and Islam as well?

Frederick II: No. There is no idea of a natural law to be found in Judaism or Islam. Their respective Laws dictate the entirety of what is necessary to live a good life. There is no other law. It is not the purpose of reason to search for guidance from the natural world or to assume the possibility of natural knowledge of ethics. The task of men is to obey the revealed Law.

Master Theodore: Following the Law for Muslims is sufficient to live a good life?

Frederick II: Yes, this suffices for the vast majority of Muslims. As Averroes says, the mass of men do not need to trouble themselves with abstruse questions about whether god's will is eternal or not, whether god is corporeal or not, or the precise manner in which they will live again after death. They need only to believe in one god and an afterlife shaped by one's earthly choice, and to follow the actions and rituals prescribed in the Law.

Master Theodore: We come back again to the difficult question: are there any grounds to prefer one of these faiths over the others?

Frederick II: Most people follow the choice of their ancestors or their community. This is unlikely to change. But you ask a different question: is one faith preferable to the others and how ought such a question be decided? Upon studying and practicing one might become convinced of the truth of one or another of these faiths. Or one might decide that each of these faiths is worthy and choose one faith on the basis of external considerations like the pleasure of a certain ritual or the way in which worship is practiced. But if you ask whether there are any rational grounds for choosing one faith over another, you are asking whether reason has the power to judge revelation. This is denied by all the faiths.

Master Theodore: There are then no reasons to prefer one faith to another?

Frederick II: As I said, one can choose a faith on practical or external grounds. One might think that one faith is better at achieving its ends than other faiths. Averroes says—at least in some of his writings—that Islam is to be preferred to Judaism and Christianity. He says that Islam's prescribed prayer rituals lead people to a deeper appreciation of god. And he says that Islam's treatment of the afterlife is preferable as well.

Master Theodore: In what way is Islam's treatment of the afterlife preferable?

Frederick II: Averroes says that its descriptions of the afterlife of the blessed and the damned are far more graphic. Its descriptions of the bodily pleasures and torments of the afterlife are more vivid and moving, and serve better to bring the mass of men to belief in god. What he says is true: the Qur'an speaks far more of the physical pleasures and agonies of the afterlife than do Judaism or Christianity. It offers to those who have chosen well a life on fine couches, served the best foods and beverages, and other ways in which perpetual happiness is enjoyed. And it describes the pains of hell for those who have strayed, including scalding water poured down throats and continual burning without end. The Qur'an speaks far more of the pains of hell than do the Christian gospels or the Torah.

Master Theodore: Is what the Qur'an says about this literally true?

Frederick II: Of course not. As Averroes says, these are simply images. They are offered to the common man who could not understand a more spiritual view of the afterlife, and in any event would not be moved by it. These images, or stories if you will, speak of physical suffering because the common man cannot conceive of any other kind of suffering. In this way, Averroes says Islam is to be preferred.

Master Theodore: This seems to establish reason's judgments as the arbiter among these faiths.

Frederick II: Yes, it does, though Averroes disguises this as much as possible.

Master Theodore: Are the prescribed actions and rituals of Islam helpful to philosophers in any way?

Frederick II: Some Islamic philosophers say that the Muslim life of practice leads best to the attainment of the theoretical virtues. This is similar to what Maimonides says about the practices and rituals of the Jewish Law.

Master Theodore: Al-Ghazali speaks differently.

Frederick II: Yes. He says that the specific rituals of Islam cannot be discovered by natural reason. Some may seem more or less arbitrary, or at least without a clear reason. But he says that their power is recognized by prophets who teach the importance of these rituals. The rituals, he says, lead far beyond reason to an ecstatic relationship with god. He says there is a vast difference between knowing truth in the manner of philosophers and living in truth as do mystics. He offers as an example that there is a wide gulf between knowing about health and actually being healthy. He says that if it is at all possible, one should try to attain this mystic consciousness oneself. If that is not possible, as it is unlikely to be for all but the rarest individuals, one should follow a prophet who has achieved this state. By this he means Muhammad. It is the quality of the true prophet to know how the proper rituals can lead to a deeper connection with god. Al-Ghazali's views, by the way, are very difficult to attack by any but the most thoughtful philosophers.

Master Theodore: By this you mean of course Averroes. What does he say about the Law?

Frederick II: Averroes says that following the Law is best for just about everyone. He says too, that in the case of philosophers, the moral virtues of Islam are the best path to the theoretical virtues, which he values above all.

Master Theodore: Does Averroes believe the moral virtues are the path to the theoretical virtues?

Frederick II: A fair question, Master Theodore. He says that the practices and moral laws of each of the faiths have much in common. While differing in specific formulations, the laws are more or less common everywhere. Where one differs in a superior way, it should be chosen. But whatever the faiths may say, there is a deep similarity among human laws in various times and places. If this is so, none of the specific laws of any of the faiths is necessary to produce good government or to live a good life. In this way, he seems to suggest that what is common to all men—which is not their faith but natural reason—might be the proper basis for human laws.

ON ETHICS AND GOVERNMENT

Master Theodore: So we must conclude that none of the three monotheistic faiths holds that man can lead a good life, or be well-governed, without their respective revelations.

Frederick II: This is true, though some like Maimonides say their Law has something of reason in it. This means that to a degree reason can approximate what is taught in the Law. But all argue that their received revelation is the path to living the best life in this world and possibly in the next as well.

Master Theodore: Must we then adopt one of the faiths in order to live well or to govern well? Can there be no ethics or government founded upon natural reason?

Frederick II: This is of course the question which Plato and Aristotle and other ancient philosophers pondered. They did so at a time before the monotheistic faiths dominated the world. They did not address the breadth of the claims of these faiths, in which faith aims to shape the laws rather than the laws shaping faith.

Master Theodore: Is there not a difference between Christianity, which has no Law, and Judaism and Islam which do?

The Papacy

Frederick II: Yes, and we shall speak of that. But first we should discuss the modern papacy, with which I have contested for many years. This is so because our popes have claimed for themselves both spiritual and temporal powers so great as to scarcely distinguish today's Christianity from the many laws of the Jews and the Muslims. There are many beliefs and practices which the church now demands. Popes have come close to saying that no one can be saved who does not follow them in all these ways.

Master Theodore: You have struggled against these practices throughout your reign.

Frederick II: Yes, I have been excommunicated three times, but I do not allow these calculated decisions of popes to threaten either my faith or my temporal position. I wish to be clear in saying that my struggles have not been against true Christian belief but against the extravagant claims of the popes. The original pure, simple theology of Christianity bears no relation to the claims of today's popes.

Master Theodore: It seems these claims have grown ever more extensive in recent years.

Frederick II: Yes, and they are now at their fullest.

Master Theodore: Discuss again how this has come to be.

Frederick II: We must go back before the time of Constantine. Even as Christians were persecuted by emperors, they grew in numbers. The result was an ever-expanding hierarchy in the church. Nowhere in scripture does it say there is to be a pope who is above all other bishops. Nor does scripture say the bishop of Rome is to be the head of the church. For many years the name "papa" or father was applied to all bishops. The bishops of Alexandria were long called "popes." The bishop of Rome was nowhere to be seen at the important Council which Constantine called at Nicaea in 325.

Master Theodore: When did this change?

Frederick II: In the late fourth century the emperor Gratian renounced the title of *Pontifex Maximus*, which had been held by emperors since Augustus. He thought this title was inappropriate for a Christian emperor. It was assumed by Damasus, who became the official as well as *de facto* head of the church. From there it was but a short step to the assertion by Gregory VII many centuries later that the title of pope can refer only to the bishop of Rome and no others.

Master Theodore: Meanwhile the papacy had acquired temporal as well as spiritual powers.

Frederick II: Yes, under the so-called Donation of Pepin the pope was granted temporal power over the region surrounding Rome. Pope Gregory VII expanded these temporal claims by asserting not only authority to excommunicate Henry IV, but also to depose him as Holy Roman Emperor. We have seen our own Gregory IX assert the same authority, which he does not legitimately exercise, over me.

Master Theodore: Gregory VII made many other innovations in the church. Many of the novel claims which he announced have come to be realized only by Gregory IX and Innocent IV in our own time.

Frederick II: Yes, the Lateran Council of 1215 has been a high water mark of the imperial papacy.

Master Theodore: You were crowned Holy Roman Emperor by Honorius. Does this imply that your powers derive from the pope?

Frederick II: I was so crowned, but it was a matter of necessity. I was raised as a young boy under the tutelage of Innocent III. I could not have obtained the title of Holy Roman Emperor without receiving it from the pope. It is also true that Charles, whom we call the Great, also received his crown from the pope. But one cannot draw conclusions about what is right from what has occurred. Emperors have also appointed and deposed popes. Do you suppose popes would regard this as a valid precedent? Emperors do not and should not depend upon popes for their rule.

Master Theodore: Do you rule then as a gift directly from god?

Frederick II: Yes, in a manner of speaking, as there is no power between me and god. My rule is not a gift from popes. Caesar did not receive his crown from Jesus. To the contrary, Caesar's rule was considered by Jesus and early Christians to be legitimate, and to which Christians should be obedient. Governmental authority is instituted from god. Paul said in Romans: "Let every person be subject to the governing authorities. For there is no authority except from God, and those that exist have been instituted by God. Therefore he who resists the authorities resists what God has appointed, and those who resist will incur judgment." And he says further: "For the same reason you also pay taxes, for the authorities are ministers of God, attending to this very thing. Pay all of them their dues, taxes to whom taxes are due, revenues to whom revenue is due, respect to whom respect is due, honor to wh social animals but also differ the most among their kind. Men have both the highest capabilities and the most destructive tendencies. Were it not for government, men would have long since annihilated themselves. Even if there were no god, government would still be founded upon necessity.

Master Theodore: You have extended this view to your subordinates as well.

Frederick II: Yes, of course. My subordinates are under my rule. The pope has no right to appoint temporal rulers, no matter how low or high their position. This is the prerogative of the emperor.

Master Theodore: Popes have argued they have the right to appoint all bishops and other clerics of the church, with no interference from the emperor.

Frederick II: This is a more difficult question. If bishops and other clerics act with no claim to temporal power, there is no reason popes should not fill these offices. This was the practice of the early church; the church chose its own leaders. When church officials began to meddle in temporal affairs, however, this created a new and different situation. To the extent that clerics aim to exercise temporal power, these positions must also be subject to the emperor and not the pope. If, as it should, the church returns to its proper spiritual focus, this would be a reasonable outcome: the church chooses its own officials and the emperor chooses those who rule with earthly power.

Master Theodore: You aimed to achieve this end in your constitution promulgated at Melfi.

Frederick II: Yes, I stripped church officials of their temporal power, their titles and their riches. Temporal powers are to be held by temporal rulers on behalf of all citizens. Church officials should then be left in peace to pursue the spiritual ends of the church.

True Christian Doctrine

Master Theodore: Church officials, including the pope, should exercise only spiritual power.

Frederick II: That is correct, and it is proper for two reasons. The first is that church officials have neither the office nor the talent to exercise temporal power. In compelling belief with temporal authority, they seem to know no bounds to their exercise of power. They pursue spiritual ends without limit or moderation. They take spiritual power far beyond what is necessary or useful for temporal rule. The three monotheistic faiths have adopted very extensive rites and practices. To enforce these with temporal power leads to very unsound results.

Master Theodore: Should the church have its own enforcement powers?

Frederick II: Abelard discusses just this question. He says the church is in an intermediate position between government and the people. He concludes the church has some enforcement powers but not those of the government. In my view the church is free to set its own standards as to who is a member and who is not. It has the power to require members to follow its rules and if they do not, to excommunicate them. The church, however, should have no power beyond that.

Master Theodore: The church should establish church doctrine, but it is for the emperor to determine how and in what ways it will be enforced.

Frederick II: Exactly so. The church may establish whatever doctrines and rites it pleases, based upon its own revelations. This is the spiritual role of the church. But it is for the emperor to decide which doctrines and rites, if any, he will choose to enforce. Men are most interesting creatures. They contest most about that which can least be known. No one attacks their fellow citizens who dispute the distance of the moon to the earth, or who contend over which is the best material with which to erect a house. Why should people kill and persecute one another over whether the universe is eternal or created? It should not be the role of emperors to punish people for that which cannot possibly be known. This is a foolish formula which creates dissension among peoples.

Master Theodore: You have taken this position clearly with regard to heresy.

Frederick II: The church may define whatever it wishes to be heresy. But it is for the emperor to punish or not to punish what the church understands as heresy. When heretical views do not threaten the peace of the people and the safety of temporal rule, why should emperors punish them? But when heretical views threaten the safety and well-being of temporal rule, they should surely be punished, as I have done on several occasions. As I have said, "heresy…shall be accounted a crime against the State, as it was in the ancient Roman laws." Heresy is not punished because it is heretical but only when it threatens the temporal order which emperors are bound to uphold.

Master Theodore: You agreed in your laws of 1232 to punish heresy.

Frederick II: Yes, my policies were aimed especially at heresies which grew up in the opposing lands of Lombardy, which were always resistant to my rule. When they aimed to export their views to my kingdom I acted against this heresy. Here I made common cause with the church, which also had its practical advantages for me.

Master Theodore: What is the second reason the church should not exercise temporal power?

Frederick II: This concerns the purity of the church itself. A church which renounces all claims to temporal power will be a simpler and purer church, far closer to the teachings of Jesus than is today's church. I spoke clearly in addressing the kings of France and England, who I believe should understand our common interest to contain the worldly power of the church. To them I said "how unlike the clergy of our day to those of the primitive church, who led apostolic lives, imitating the humility of the Lord." Can you imagine Jesus or his disciples enriching themselves and claiming the right to appoint and depose emperors?

Master Theodore: Jesus himself spoke about this.

Frederick II: When asked about temporal power Jesus was very clear. He said "render to Caesar the things that are Caesar's, and to God the things that are God's." And Peter said "Be subject to every human institution, whether it be to the emperor as supreme, or to governors sent by him to punish those who do wrong and praise those who do right … Honor all men. Love the brotherhood. Fear God. Honor the emperor." What has today's papacy to do with any of these sentiments?

Master Theodore: Today's church has abandoned the original simplicity of true Christian doctrine.

Frederick II: Today's popes seek riches, they seek titles and they seek control of the temporal world. They say it is the purpose of the emperor to do their bidding. None of these practices are to be found in either the teachings or the example of Jesus. They are at complete variance with them.

Master Theodore: It was a long path to this point.

Frederick II: As we have discussed, the reign of Constantine was a turning point in the history of the church. It was well that Constantine should end the persecution of the church. But the temptation of the church then to exercise its own imperial power was too great. We see already in the fourth century the great increase in men like Antony and Hilarion, who rejected the growing worldliness of the imperial church in favor of a purer asceticism. This we see right up to the present day.

Master Theodore: This was the inspiration of your acquaintance Francis, who was from Assisi.

Frederick II: Yes, Francis aimed to bring the church back to its earlier simple purity. He wished, as do I, to see a church which is purer, poorer and humbler. This would greatly benefit the church's true spiritual mission.

Master Theodore: Francis, however, found some favor in the church with his radical doctrines.

Frederick II: Yes, he was more careful than other sects which, having many of the same ends, have been declared heretical. Francis came close to heresy in the eyes of the church, but managed to fall short of it because he was willing to work within the church. He did not contradict the notion that obeying the pope is the best guarantee of salvation.

Master Theodore: Can true faith be compelled by the temporal power?

Frederick II: This is an attractive tool for thoughtless church leaders. It rarely accomplishes its goal. There are better tools to advance the spiritual ends of the church. The main one is of course persuasion. This includes both reasoned arguments and graphic representations of the consequences of belief and unbelief. But there is no more powerful tool than living a life as an example of Jesus' teachings. This accounts for the extraordinary growth of the early church.

Master Theodore: It seems, then, that one can find in the original purity of Christian doctrine what is lacking in Judaism and Islam: a space for government to act separately from the Laws of faith. In this way government does not derive its legitimacy or its purposes from revelation.

Frederick II: Yes, for the Jews and Muslims it is very different. Josephus, for example, says that Moses ordained the government of the Jews to be a theocracy. That is, it rested not upon the claims of men but upon the Law of god promulgated by Moses. It is much the same with the Muslims.

But today's popes work day and night to remove this independence. There was from the beginning an opening in Christianity which is not found in Judaism or Islam. This was true of Jesus himself, who claimed no power to rule in the temporal sphere. Jesus was not the messiah the Jews imagined, who would free them from Roman rule and allow them to re-establish after many years their own government. Until the reign of Constantine there was a clear separation of the ends of the church and the ends of government.

Master Theodore: It seems too that Christianity has provided from the beginning a similar space for reflection on the nature and proper ends of government which is lacking in Judaism and Islam.

Frederick II: This is well said, Master Theodore: Christianity has indeed provided an opening, so to say, for reflection on the ends of government. This we see from the earliest times. In the fourth century Augustine, for example, wrote extensively on the purpose and ends of temporal power. Christian thinkers were in this way more open to the political thinking of the ancients. The Arabs learned much from the ancient writers about medicine, law, biology, and mathematics, but with the exception of rare thinkers like al-Farabi and Averroes they found little of use in ancient political thought. To speak of the ends of temporal government Christian thinkers had to have recourse to the question of the nature and ends of man. In this way, the question of man's nature arose in a way it did not in Judaism and Islam. There we find very little idea of man's "nature."

Master Theodore: As we have discussed, many of today's Christian thinkers have been led to explore whether there is such a thing as "natural law," that is, knowledge of man's ends—or ethics—that can be known by natural reason, unaided by revelation.

Frederick II: In this way these recent Christian thinkers have been led back to the questions of ancient political philosophy, that is, what can we know of man's ends and man's governance.

Master Theodore: This explains why we see the idea of natural law developing in Christianity.

Frederick II: Yes, but also for another related reason. The teaching of Jesus was simple to state: love god and love your neighbor. This is far easier to reconcile with natural reason than are the complexities of the revealed Law.

Master Theodore: Could we say then that Christianity is a faith which is closer to philosophy than Judaism or Islam?

Frederick II: An interesting question, Master Theodore. Can one faith be more consistent with philosophy than others? Is Christianity more consistent with philosophy than other faiths? The answer is both yes and no. It is certainly harder to reconcile Christianity with philosophy because of its complicated triune god. And all the more so since this god took on a human form. This is very much at odds with the spiritual and largely unknowable god of the philosophers. The simple monotheism of Judaism and Islam are closer to the god of philosophy. On the other hand, the absence of the Law in Christianity certainly offers space for reflection on man's ends and the ends of his institutions, so far as these can be known by natural reason.

Models of Government

Master Theodore: These thoughts lead us directly to our most pressing question: can ethics or good governance be based on natural reason, without the aid of revelation?

Frederick II: To know whether men can lead good or ethical lives and create good government one must know what is man's nature. Without this knowledge ethics consists of little more than empty preaching. The best life is one in which man's nature is best fulfilled. As has been said by wise men, the ends are not for the creature, but the creature is for his ends. So too with government. Without knowledge of man's nature it is not possible to speak of what is good government. Absent direct revelations from god, such knowledge is the only way to understand the proper ends of government.

Master Theodore: Where can we learn the ends of men and government?

Frederick II: Three models have been proposed to understand the ends of government. One is through knowledge of the stars. Plato was not the first but was certainly the most important thinker to suggest that knowledge of the stars and knowledge of the ends of human institutions must go together. He said in *Timaeus* that man's ends should be in alignment with the stars.

Master Theodore: What does this mean?

Frederick II: Man is a creature of the cosmos, as are the stars. Both are ensouled, which is to say that they have power to move themselves. If by this Plato means that man must find his meaning in the cosmos then I see no objection to that.

Master Theodore: Plato seemed to suggest more than this. He seemed to suggest that man must order his actions according to what he knows of the motion of the stars.

Frederick II: Yes, this is what we call today by the name of astrology. There is nothing wrong in principle in seeking to order our actions by considering what we can learn of the stars, that is, of the natural world which surrounds us. Learning from the nature of the cosmos within which we live may be helpful to orient our actions. But this study has produced very little useful knowledge in practice. To say that we should align ourselves with the cosmos is well and good, but what follows from this? If the stars move in circles or some other regular path, what does this tell us about our lives and our choices? If planets come together in the sky, how does this affect our lives? In *Timaeus* Plato also said that human beings and the broader cosmos are very different from one another in important ways. Human beings are buffeted about by "sensations" in a way in which the cosmos is not, as there is nothing outside the cosmos.

Master Theodore: You employ astrologers, however, do you not?

Frederick II: I see nothing to be lost by this. But I pay little attention in practice to the predictions of astrologers. I tested Michael Scot on one occasion.

Master Theodore: What did you learn from this?

Frederick II: I learned that it is quite possible to measure accurate distances in the cosmos. This I found to be very impressive. But I did not learn anything about how to conduct my life or to administer my empire. Michael Scot says "the heavenly bodies are not the cause of events, but the sign thereof, as the compasses in front of the tavern are the sign that wine is within."

Master Theodore: We can measure the stars but we cannot learn how to act from them.

Frederick II: Yes, in this way I agree with the three monotheistic faiths. These faiths are deeply skeptical of the practice of astrology. If knowledge of the stars could teach us how to live, why would we need the church or the Law? If we could learn ethics from the stars, why would we need revelation at all? We could know good and evil without any revelation from god.

Mater Theodore: So human justice is not a mirror of cosmic justice?

Frederick II: Both might be called doing what the ensouled capability of each enables it to do. But I see no more specific and useful analogy than that. What I see instead are foolish and unwarranted analogies that the pope is like the sun and the emperor like the moon. This argument itself is extremely weak; the light of the moon derives from the sun's light but the moon itself does not derive from the sun. Popes do not create emperors, which by the way long antedated popes. Upon what, really, are such notions which the popes advance founded? There is nothing in nature to support any of this.

Master Theodore: We are unlikely to learn the ends of government by studying the stars.

Frederick II: Plato proposed a second model by which to understand government. He said in the *Republic* that the ends of government and individual men could be understood in terms of one another. He said the human soul and government are models for one another.

Master Theodore: What do you think of this analogy?

Frederick II: I agree that one should consider carefully the nature of the human soul. Plato said the soul is composed of three parts, or qualities, which he called reasoning, spirited and appetitive. He said these qualities are found in different proportions among people. This is a useful way to look at the soul, though it is by no means the only way to do so. Plato said, and in this he is followed by Aristotle, that the true and best end of men is to fulfill the capabilities of their soul. Both philosophers said—though this too is not necessarily so—that to fulfill the part of the soul which is unique to men, reason, is the most complete fulfillment. Though not unreasonable, there is nothing logically entailed about this.

Master Theodore: Can such a soul be a model for government?

Frederick II: Government is very different than individual men. Can one say that if the end of individual men is to give full play to their reason, that one has learned anything at all about the ends of government? Should the purpose of government be to protect and advance the few who are most capable of reasoning? Or to cause every citizen to reason better, even if only by a little and unevenly?

Master Theodore: Like the stars, individual men are different than government.

Frederick II: They have in common that they exist but little else.

Master Theodore: There is a third model for government, as you say, and this concerns the arts and crafts.

Frederick II: Yes, this model for government was also proposed by Plato. Just as the end of the craftsman is to do well at his craft, it is the end of government to do so as well. Fair enough, but what have we learned from this? We can know a helmsman is a good helmsman if he steers his ship safely to port. We can know a good shoemaker if he makes shoes which are admired by their wearer. A good government must achieve its proper ends, to be sure, but what do these ends have to do with those of a helmsman or a shoemaker? The helmsman's craft is a technical one, and his goal is set by the ship's owner. But who is the owner of government? The ruler, some of the citizens or all of the citizens? A shoemaker's goodness is determined by the owner who finds the shoes good and useful. But who is the owner of government? Is it the emperor, a class of men or all men? These matters we cannot learn from analogies to helmsmen and shoemakers.

Master Theodore: These analogies by which to understand government do not seem very helpful, unless they are designed to prove a point determined in advance.

Frederick II: It does not help to learn the ends of government by looking everywhere except at government itself. What can be said is that government has something to do with the ends of men, but one must reason very carefully from that and not take refuge in unfounded analogies. To know the various ends of men, and therefore man's nature is only a necessary and not a sufficient condition to know the ends of government.

Frederick II: We have spoken about the opening which Christianity provided to reflect on man's nature and the ends of government. Augustine, for example, offers a view of government like this.

Frederick II: Yes, Augustine says government is a punishment for man's sinfulness. He says that before man's fall into evil no government was needed; government is god's punishment for man's sinfulness.

Master Theodore: Do you agree with Augustine?

Frederick II: No, I do not. Augustine says there are two types of man, one before and one after the fall. This view is not derived from natural reason, but from revelation. If we are to find a basis for government in natural reason, we must exclude this view and look elsewhere. Moreover, how long did Adam exist in his presumed pre-fall condition? Very briefly, it seems, and certainly before other men were present. It is of course true to say that when only Adam and Eve existed, government was not required. This is to say very little. Man in his pre-fall condition had no knowledge of good and evil and it is difficult to see what we can learn of ethics and government from such a supposed state of affairs. Moreover, if at his very first chance man sins by seeking to know good and evil, can we not say that this is likely to have been his true nature all along?

Master Theodore: Where does Augustine err?

Frederick II: He errs in seeing sinfulness as man's principal quality. To see men in such a way is possible only if one contrasts men as they are with an imaginary picture of man, which is not drawn from careful analysis but from revelation. He sees the entire role of government to punish sinful behavior

Master Theodore: In your introduction to the constitution you promulgate in the *Liber Augustalis* you seem to offer a picture of sinful man similar to Augustine.

Frederick II: So it seems on the surface, but not in a deeper way. Of course, as we will discuss, it is part of government's role to maintain order and to deal with offenders. But government should not be viewed as a punishment for man's condition, but as a means for men to lead the most fulfilled lives. Aristotle has the better view; he considers man as he is, not through the lens of revelation. Everywhere one finds men one finds governments; government is natural to man, not a punishment from god for rejecting his pre-fall nature. If god wished to punish men he could have found better and more effective ways to do this directly than to institute governments. Man is indeed self-interested—sinful, if you wish to call it that—but he also needs government by his very social nature. Man is, as Aristotle says, inclined to exist together with his fellow men and to create institutions and practices to improve his life. The ends of government are not entirely negative but are positive as well. It would be better to say that government is a gift from god, not a punishment.

Master Theodore: The ends of government, then, are to be discovered neither in unfounded analogies nor in an assumed condition of man which, if it existed at all, was passingly brief.

Frederick II: We can learn the ends of government only by considering what purpose men find in it. This cannot be found by looking at the stars, or human arts and crafts, or an imagined tri-partite soul. It means looking at government itself.

The Ends of Government

Master Theodore: What then are the ends of government, and how might we judge between good and bad governments? It is often said that the true end of government is the common good.

Frederick II: Plato goes further, saying that each citizen doing what he does best will achieve the common good. We might agree that the common good is the true end of government. But this in itself tells us very little. The common good is not an idea to be found lying at hand which it is our task to discover. The common good, or some approximation to it, must be uncovered by discerning what are the ends of actual people, the goods of people which can actually be achieved. We cannot do this in our head—as we might do mathematics—but must rather see what people need and desire, and draw from this a path forward. Moreover, it does not help much in this quest to say that each citizen should do only what he does best. There is no reason to think there is one specific role or task for each person, which should then be imposed upon him. Citizens may have several or more ends and also several sets of skills. I know several languages better than my translators. Should I then be a translator and not an emperor? I can be both.

Master Theodore: Is there then no such thing as the common good?

Frederick II: I do not say this. I say only that what is good depends upon observing actual governments and discovering what their ends might be. In this way we can determine whether there are ends which are common to all governments, ends at which all governments must aim in order to succeed. We will not find a pattern for this laid up in heaven, but only through careful observation of actual governments. If there are ends at which all governments aim, we can then consider which governments most successfully achieve these ends.

Master Theodore: What are the ends at which all governments aim? Do they aim to benefit all citizens equally, or to benefit some more than others? Do they aim to benefit the rulers or all citizens? Should the ruler be an emperor, the few or the many?

Frederick II: These are questions which cannot be answered abstractly. Much depends upon the circumstances in which governments find themselves.

Master Theodore: We cannot say then that a kingship or an aristocracy or rule by the citizens themselves is the best form of government?

Frederick II: No. It is my view that rule by an emperor is best, but the quality of government does not depend as much upon its form as upon the quality of its ruler. One could even imagine a more or less good form of democratic government, but only if it is guided by reasonable principles established by its founders. In and of itself a democracy could be either good or bad. If the people rule themselves in accord with the guidance of wise founders it may be acceptable. But democracies seem to have a very difficult time restraining themselves in this way, and often give themselves over to whatever is desired at the moment. This becomes self-defeating and no one's ends are well-served. That is why I favor government by a king or emperor. But here too kings and emperors must be wise to be successful.

Master Theodore: Speak further about Augustine's idea that government is god's punishment for man's sinfulness.

Frederick II: Such a government would have as its only end to preserve order. Order must of course be preserved, but this is too narrow a view. This is to see government in an altogether negative way. As I will propose, governments have broader, more positive ends than this. Augustine's view sees only the sinful nature of fallen man, but there is more to man than this.

Master Theodore: How extensive then are the ends of government?

Frederick II: There is a careful balance to be found here. The ends of Augustine's earthly government are too narrow. But it is also surely true that the ends of the three monotheistic faiths are far too extensive for the ends of temporal government. To use Augustine's language, we might say that temporal governments which aim to impose revelation on their citizens are trying to bring the city of god to the earth, which is not possible.

Master Theodore: Does Plato make this mistake?

Frederick II: It is said that in his *Laws* Plato establishes hundreds of very specific and detailed laws in instituting his proposed government. This is foolish. The ends of government must be neither too high nor too low.

Master Theodore: Might we say then that Plato makes the same error as do the three monotheistic faiths which aim to impose the commands of their revealed faith?

Frederick II: Yes, though in a different way. And one might ask what experience Plato had regarding the constitution and maintenance of actual governments. So far as I know, he never ruled over anyone, as I do. And so far as I know, his prescriptions for government were never followed by any actual ruler. He aimed, but failed, to institute a new government for Sicily; I have actually done this. Plato's record regarding governance seems marked by bad choices and failures at each step of his life. Plato's philosophy offers much to ponder, as I will discuss. But his ideas concerning government, whether ideal or actual, seem to me of little use. We must look at actual governments to determine the ends of government.

Master Theodore: What then are the ends of government?

Frederick II: There are—as the ancient Romans knew—two ends which seem always to be present in government, and according to how well these ends are achieved we can measure good and bad governments. These two ends are *Pax* and *Justitia.* These we see by looking at actual governments, not by elaborate and fanciful analogies with the stars, human arts and crafts or the structure of the human soul.

Master Theodore: Let us speak then about peace and justice.

Frederick II: Of these *Pax* (peace) is the first, both in logical order and in importance. By peace I mean more than the establishment of order by force. The establishment of order is important but it does not describe the fullness of true peace. Force is required to impose order, to be sure. But peace is more than punishing crimes to preserve order.

Master Theodore: What more is included in peace?

Frederick II: True peace requires the creation of a state in which citizens are not driven by the laws themselves to create offenses. In like manner, true peace requires more than defeating foreign enemies on the battlefield; it requires actions to protect against the possibility of foreign attack. True peace exists only where there is a reasonable expectation of order so that citizens' many human ends can be successfully pursued.

Master Theodore: Peace is necessary to all citizens then?

Frederick II: Yes. Only those who live in a time and place who can take peace for granted will fail to understand its importance. Those who live without peace know better. Without peace it is difficult or impossible for men to pursue their many ends, whatever they may be. Without peace can men grow crops for their subsistence? Can men learn to hunt with falcons? Can philosophers pursue wisdom without peace? Peace is the condition which allows men to pursue their ends, both contemplative and practical. Peace not only permits but encourages human fulfillment.

Master Theodore: How is peace best achieved?

Frederick II: Wise rulers must consider many factors, as we shall discuss. But as a general matter it is best preserved by the promulgation of laws. Laws provide predictability for human choices; they allow citizens to pursue their ends in a framework which can be understood and acted upon with confidence. The laws may vary from place to place and from time to time, as necessity may require. But to speak generally the laws must be clear, well-known and without unpredictable changes.

Master Theodore: Are some laws better than others?

Frederick II: Again, much depends upon circumstances, which wise rulers must recognize. But the best laws are those which establish *Justitia* (justice).

Master Theodore: Why are just laws best?

Frederick II: Just laws are best because they are necessary to establish and preserve true peace. As we say in the *Liber Augustalis*, "respect for peace cannot exist apart from justice and apart from which justice cannot exist." We say further that peace and justice "embrace each other like twin sisters." If there is no justice, there will be no true peace.

Master Theodore: Of what then are just laws comprised?

Frederick II: Again, much depends upon circumstances that wise rulers must address. But to speak generally, justice consists in treating citizens in a way which is fitting for them.

Master Theodore: Does this mean that just laws must treat all citizens equally?

Frederick II: In one way, yes. All people have some claim upon the law in so far as they are citizens. The ancient Romans spoke wisely of citizens' "equality under the law." A government in which citizens have no claim under the law would not be just. As we announced in our *Liber Augustalis*, for example, "we cannot allow Jews and Saracens to be defrauded of the power of our protection because a difference of religion renders them hateful and deprives them of all other help."

Master Theodore: Are all people then to be treated the same?

Frederick II: This does not follow. People are also unequal to one another in many ways. This too must be considered. Aristotle spoke most wisely when he said that people who are equal in one way should not assume they are equal in all ways. Justice does not require that people be treated equally in all ways. Much depends upon circumstances and upon the ways in which a given people are unequal. The laws must recognize, for example, that some citizens are large property owners and others are not. It is not the purpose of the law to create equality in property. This kind of scheme, such as Plato proposed in his *Republic*, will itself be unjust and the proof of this is that it will inevitably destroy peace. Differences between citizens' wealth, their property, their social standing and their virtue must be accommodated by just laws. Some may benefit more, but they may also pay more. As we have promulgated in our *Liber Augustalis*, citizens of higher standing and more wealth must pay higher fines than poorer citizens for the same infractions of the law. And it is not reasonable to impose the same burden of taxation upon the poor as upon the wealthy.

Master Theodore: Are the wealthier, the nobler and the more intelligent then to be treated altogether differently than other citizens?

Frederick II: No. Aristotle also says that people who are unequal in one way should not assume they are unequal in all ways.

Master Theodore: How then are we to know the ways in which citizens should be treated equally and the ways in which they should be treated unequally?

Frederick II: This cannot be said absolutely, but depends upon circumstances. If there is a kingdom in which the nobles have traditionally enjoyed many advantages, it would be foolish to try to abolish them all at once. This would bring a speedy end to peace and therefore could not be just. Nor should a wise ruler attempt to create new classes of advantages among citizens who have traditionally regarded one another as largely equal.

Master Theodore: Who is to judge in these matters of justice?

Frederick II: You are asking who should rule. Certain ancient Athenians believed the citizens should rule themselves. As we have discussed, a democratic form of government might survive for a time if it is wise enough to bind itself to the laws laid down for them by intelligent founders. But when democracies break away from wise laws and govern themselves as they please, they are unlikely to survive very long. Justice depends less on the form of government than on the wisdom of those who rule.

It is my judgment that rule by emperors is the best way to achieve peace and justice. For many reasons, emperors are wiser than the mass of men, who as a rule do not seek wisdom and thus are not well able to secure the blessings of peace and justice.

Master Theodore: Are you speaking then of what Plato called kings who are philosophers?

Frederick II: It is true that rulers who think deeply about how to achieve peace and justice will be better rulers. How could it be otherwise? But Plato speaks as if there is a perfect model of peace and justice, rather than many versions of it. A wise ruler must of course understand the ends of government, which are peace and justice. But he must also possess practical wisdom as well as contemplative wisdom if he is to succeed. Here I agree with what both Averroes and Maimonides have said; wise rulers must possess both demonstrative, or philosophical wisdom and cogitative, or practical wisdom. These qualities they find in their respective prophets. But here I disagree with them, because it is the purpose of prophets to reveal what god has revealed to them, not simply to seek peace and justice. This is why popes are ill-suited as temporal rulers. They are not prophets, as must be apparent to all, but like the prophets of Judaism and Islam they fail to comprehend that the ends of temporal government are peace and justice, not the imposition of revelation.

Master Theodore: If an emperor or any other ruler establishes the laws, are they bound by these laws?

Frederick II: In the first instance, yes. But the ruling authority in any government always retains the power to change the law itself. Thus they are not in this way ultimately bound by their own laws, which they can change if it seems wise or necessary to do so. But a good ruler will always keep a careful eye to achieve peace and justice, even when changing the laws. As I have said, "Although our illustriousness is free of every law, yet it is not exalted above the dictates of Reason, herself the mother of all Law." Reason is the mother of *Pax* and *Justitia*, her two inseparable daughters. Rulers understand that they can change the laws. This is the problem of democracies: so long as they do not act on their intrinsic freedom to change the laws they have a chance to succeed. But when democracies lose the respect they have for their unchanging constitution moderation gives way license.

Master Theodore: If I understand you correctly, you are saying that revelation is not necessary to shape good government, but that good government can be achieved by natural reason.

Frederick II: This is what the wisest men believe. Averroes, for example, says reason teaches that good governments do not aim too high or too low. He says in such governments we often see certain common features among the laws of all peoples. The temporal ends of government are peace and justice and these can be apprehended, in principle and largely in practice, by natural reason. The complex and detailed ends of governments which are founded on revelation do not have this character.

The Means of Government

Master Theodore: Let us speak now of what natural reason can teach us about how to govern in order to achieve peace and justice. If practical reason is to guide us, there must be at least some rules for how to achieve peace and justice. These may depend to a degree upon circumstances, but must there not be broad guidance from natural reason?

Frederick II: A fair question, Master Theodore. As we have discussed, much depends upon circumstances and flexibility to change the laws to meet these circumstances. Indeed, I would put this as the first of three practical rules to achieve good government: necessity must temper a good ruler's actions. By this I mean that whatever long-term conditions a good ruler may think useful to achieve peace and justice, he must act in accord with the circumstances he confronts.

Master Theodore: This sounds eminently reasonable, but please clarify your meaning.

Frederick II: As emperor it is my goal to unite all of the kingdoms of Europe under one rule, as was the case with the Roman emperors of old. But this is not possible today and to try to achieve it all at once would be folly. There would be no peace. That is why I have consistently honored the prerogatives of the French and English kings. This has been necessary in order to allow me to address the more urgent problems I confront with today's popes. I have at every turn reminded the French and English kings of their need to make common cause against the overreaching of popes.

Master Theodore: The same is true of how you have dealt with the German nobles and those of Sicily.

Frederick II: Yes, the German nobles are deeply embedded in their territories and I do not have the ability to change this. It would be a mistake to attempt to impose upon the German nobles the same laws I have imposed upon Sicilian nobles, where I have a freer hand. It is my view that the people of Germany would benefit from a more centralized, more reasoned form of rule which eliminates the personal power of the German nobles, but that is not possible to achieve today. Peace would be the first casualty of any such attempt. Boethius has wisely said that "it takes very little to spoil the perfect happiness of the fortunate."

Master Theodore: Speak about your policy toward Sicily, which you set forth most clearly in your *Liber Augustalis* issued at Melfi.

Frederick II: Here I have had a freer hand to construct a lasting basis for peace and justice. I have been able to reduce the power of local nobles to a certain extent, replacing their personal and arbitrary rule with laws for the entire kingdom. It is my view that justice is better served if administered by a emperor who follows established laws and procedures. When nobles exercise their personal prerogatives over citizens and against one another, we find scores settled in the most narrow and unpredictable ways. Emotion and family advantage, rather than reason, lead noble families to run amok with their power. It is far more conducive to peace and justice to have authority located with an emperor who takes a larger and longer view than we find in the endless provocations and disputes which bedevil our noble families.

Master Theodore: Even in Sicily, however, you draw some distinctions between the nobles and ordinary citizens.

Frederick II: Yes, this too is governed by necessity and not by my preference. As you know, I abolished trial by combat to settle disputes. Trial by combat settles disputes by combat between contesting parties or by champions who are hired to fight on their behalf. Reason teaches that this is no way to settle disputes; outcomes depend not on justice but on the physical strength of the combatants, which is in no way the same. But as you know, I have permitted this practice for a small class of nobles, for whom it would have been impossible in practice to abolish it. At least in these cases trial by combat is preferable to full-scale war between entire principalities.

Master Theodore: These are decisions driven by reason.

Frederick II: Yes, but only in the sense that reason teaches it is unwise to wage war against necessity. It is my view that it best suits the ends of peace and justice for all citizens to secure their rights from a common source, not from a patchwork of differing and unpredictable sources. We have seen this best accomplished by the remarkable Augustus, who ruled over the most extended period of peace and justice the world has ever seen. But practical wisdom must teach what is possible to achieve in actual circumstances.

Master Theodore: Wise rulers must decide, then, where reason can prevail directly and where it must adapt itself to necessity.

Frederick II: Yes. Let me illustrate further. A wise ruler has considerable latitude. He may decide to expand the borders of his realm, which can affect the security, the finances and the well-being of his realm. Rulers can change tariff and taxation laws, depending upon the financial health of the realm. Rulers can alter punishments which are prescribed for crimes against the realm. Rulers have wide discretion in these and many other similar matters.

Master Theodore: Are there limits to the discretion of rulers?

Frederick II: Yes, we have discussed the fact that rulers must recognize and not vainly oppose necessity. Speaking generally, we may say that a ruler should not impose large and sweeping changes on a people which is not prepared for them. For example, I have abolished trial by ordeal in my realm. Trial by ordeal is not based upon reason; guilty or innocent defendants do not sink or swim because of their guilt or innocence, but as a result of physical properties. As I have asked, "How could a man believe that the natural heat of glowing iron will become cool or cold without an adequate cause? Or that, because of a seared conscience, the element of cold water will refuse to accept the accused?" Trial by ordeal is contrary to reason. I was able to abolish this practice, which was long established, because the Lateran Council of 1215 prepared the ground by condemning trial by ordeal for its own reasons.

Master Theodore: You have spoken of three rules of practical reason to achieve the ends of peace and justice. What is the second of these rules?

Frederick II: Here we must speak again of the question of religious faith. I have said that it is not the role of the emperor to be a handmaiden to the pope. Emperors do not derive their power from popes. But this does not mean there is no role for faith under a government which pursues peace and justice. Far from it.

Master Theodore: Please explain your meaning.

Frederick II: There must be some common set of beliefs among citizens in order to guarantee peace. However wise a ruler, it is not possible to achieve peace if the great majority of citizens does not hold a set of beliefs in common.

Master Theodore: A common faith is one such set of beliefs.

Frederick II: Yes, faith is not the only way to achieve this, but it is the most common and often the most effective way.

Master Theodore: Plato speaks about this in both his ideal state and in the practical rules of his *Laws*.

Frederick II: Yes, in the *Laws* Plato says citizens must hold three minimal beliefs: that there are gods, that the gods care for men, and that the gods cannot be bribed by rituals or prayers. Maimonides speaks somewhat similarly.

Master Theodore: What is Plato's meaning?

Frederick II: If citizens do not believe there are gods who watch over men, men will assume they can do anything with impunity. This would destroy the foundation of both peace and justice. And if citizens believe they can shape events by their rituals or prayers, this would suggest that they control the gods rather than the gods control them. This too is a formula for license which undermines the foundation of peace and justice.

Master Theodore: Do you follow Plato in his views?

Frederick II: Yes, although the common faith which undergirds peace and justice can be achieved in a number of ways. Plato offers these three beliefs as the minimum necessary for good government. There may be broader or deeper or more detailed common beliefs. Plato never witnessed faiths with the deep roots of the three monotheisms which prescribe many specific beliefs and practices.

Master Theodore: Can there be common beliefs which do not depend upon the gods?

Frederick II: It is possible, but not easy. Wise rulers can go some distance to provide order in such a situation, but it is very difficult. This is a special problem for democratic governments. It is very difficult for the mass of men to hold to a steady and moderate course if they do not believe there are gods who watch over them and punish their excesses, in this world or the next. It is likely that such a government will be only temporary; when the people discover they have no rulers but themselves they are likely to adopt new practices which will destroy the foundation of peace and justice.

Master Theodore: What are the common beliefs of your empire?

Frederick II: Christianity provides a common set of beliefs for all of Europe.

Master Theodore: Christianity then is indispensable for peace and justice in Europe?

Frederick II: Given the history of Europe since the end of the ancient Roman empire, yes, Christianity has played this role.

Master Theodore: Might it have been different?

Frederick II: Of course. Muslim armies might have conquered all of Europe. In that case Islam would have provided a common set of beliefs, as it does now in the lands of the east and northern Africa.

Master Theodore: Is one set of common beliefs better than another?

Frederick II: Theologians and faithful believers would answer in the affirmative. Each of the three monotheistic faiths offers arguments for why its beliefs and practices are best. But here I am speaking not of the truth of these beliefs but of their usefulness to achieve the temporal ends of peace and justice.

Master Theodore: Can any set of common beliefs achieve this purpose? Can citizens believe anything at all, so long as it is held in common?

Frederick II: A fair question, Master Theodore. There are bounds to what can succeed as a common set of beliefs. A common set of beliefs cannot run directly against what reason teaches is the nature of men. For example, the communism of Plato's ideal state will never succeed. Men always favor what is close to them, what is their own. They will never be content with the abstract ideal of communism. That is why Plato must propose a complex and all-embracing set of lies to support such a government. But even this will not be sufficient against the power of natural human inclination. This proposed government and its necessary lies are against reason.

Master Theodore: You support the common beliefs of Christianity in your empire.

Frederick II: Yes. We have difficulty enough achieving peace with this common set of beliefs. It would be far worse without them. Imagine to yourself a kingdom or an empire with equal shares of Christians, Muslims and Jews. Do you suppose it would be easy, or even possible, to secure peace in such a situation? It has never been my intent to attack Christian beliefs, but only the exaggerated claims of the popes, which themselves endanger peace.

Master Theodore: However, you tolerate both Muslim and Jewish beliefs in your empire.

Frederick II: Yes. These beliefs are marginal in our empire. They are no threat to the common beliefs of Christianity in our empire. When the Muslims in Sicily opposed my rule, however, this was different; I quickly put down their rebellion. I moved the pacified Muslim population to Lucera on the Italian mainland, and since then they have been strong supporters of my rule. And the Jews have always been a marginal people in Europe, who offer no threat to our empire. For these reasons I tolerate both faiths. I have no interest to persecute views which do not threaten the peace of the empire.

Master Theodore: It seems that your policies toward Christian heretics are harsher than your policies toward Muslims and Jews.

Frederick II: This is true. Heresy undermines the common set of Christian beliefs which undergird peace. If these views are expressed randomly here and there, they are of no consequence. If they are held in the private thoughts of men—as Constantine urged his disputatious bishops to do—they threaten no one. But the heresies with which I am concerned are imported into our empire by my opponents, such as arise in Lombardy and southern France. Here I make common cause with the church. I have been baptized into the common beliefs of Christianity. It is my task to watch over and protect the church, so long as this does not injure my royal rights. When I can, I support the common beliefs of the church. But as I have said many times, it is for the temporal power and not the church to decide when heresy constitutes a threat to temporal rule and thus must be punished.

Master Theodore: Will Christianity always make up the common beliefs of Europe?

Frederick II: It is difficult to predict the future, which I leave to my astrologers. But what is easier to say is this: rulers should never attempt lightly to change the common beliefs of people. This will never go well. If a ruler took it into his mind to replace long-standing Christian beliefs with, say, Muslim beliefs this would not succeed without great violence and the destruction of peace. We have witnessed this when Muslim armies have captured Christian lands and imposed upon them the beliefs of Islam. This cannot succeed without violent conquest. If a ruler took it into his mind to alter Christian beliefs in a radical way, this too would lead to violence and the destruction of peace. One must preserve if at all possible the deeply held ancient beliefs of a people.

The task of temporal rule is not to change the religious beliefs of a people, but to preserve peace and justice.

Master Theodore: Your second practical rule of governing also seems wise. What is the third practical rule which reason teaches to create and maintain peace and justice?

Frederick II: Here is a subject close to my heart. The third practical rule to achieve good government is education.

Master Theodore: Do you mean education in theological matters?

Frederick II: No, this is the province of the church. It is for the church to establish such education for its priests and its believers as it sees fit. This is a matter for the church and it is for the church to create and maintain—and I should also say finance—such educational institutions as it finds useful. Such education is not to compel anyone, but to create a path for the transmission of the church's doctrines.

Master Theodore: You speak then of secular education. What kinds of education are useful to preserve and enhance peace and justice?

Frederick II: I speak mainly of matters which are practical and not theoretical. Those who are inclined to philosophy will find their way without special institutions. This has surely been true of me, for I have studied no course of philosophy beyond what I have sought out for myself. There is no need for a large class of philosophers to preserve peace and government. It is enough that rulers are oriented toward reason, both theoretical and, as we are speaking of now, practical.

Master Theodore: Discuss what types of education are important for good government.

Frederick II: Let me speak first of the law. Christian theologians have long taught canon law, the rules according to which the church operates. I have aimed to create a new study of law which is not based upon church doctrine but on man's reason. I have looked back to ancient Roman law as a guide, but have also aimed to improve it where it is needed. As you know, I founded the University of Naples in 1224 for this very purpose, among others. Peace and justice are best secured by a class of legal administrators who are familiar with the means and the ends of law. This generates a degree of impartiality, predictability and order, which we do not find among either theocratic governments or the rule of nobles in their local territories.

Master Theodore: Can this knowledge be taught and learned like any other craft?

Frederick II: Yes, when the ends of peace and justice are established by wise rulers, it is possible to learn specific precedents and procedures by which justice can be administered through the laws.

Master Theodore: This seems a very new idea.

Frederick II: It is better to say that it is a re-discovery of an old idea. The University of Naples was the first of what I hope will be many such institutions. It is from there that I draw much legal talent to administer my kingdom in Sicily.

Master Theodore: Can this new class of legal administers generate justice by themselves?

Frederick II: They are a means to this end. But they too depend for the administration of justice on a ruler who has the ends of peace and justice always clearly in mind. Without such a ruler, this class of administrators can also lose their way and administer laws to their own advantage rather than that of the entire kingdom. The goal is to end all private settlement of accounts, both for the administrators and for all citizens.

Master Theodore: You have also proposed reforms to the practice of medicine.

Frederick II: Yes. Although this is less vital than the laws, it is also important. I have established laws to ensure that those who practice medicine are capable to do it well. Physicians must be trained in medicine and tested on their knowledge before they can practice medicine. Without this training and evaluation, it is illegal to practice medicine in my kingdom. This ensures not only better health for citizens—a goal which all share—but also reduces disputes and even revenge taken against physicians who are not competent. Where it is possible to establish clear and effective rules to guide those arts which serve the citizens, they should be established.

Master Theodore: Are there other areas of education which you favor?

Frederick II: Yes, I favor the teaching and study of all aspects of the natural world. For this reason I have ordered the many translations of important works I have commissioned to be shared widely with all universities, including Bologna and my own university at Naples. Despite Bologna's longstanding opposition to my rule, I wrote them some years back: "We have always loved knowledge from our youth; whatever time we can steal from state affairs we cheerfully dedicate to reading the many volumes stored in our library. We have stripped the works written by the Greek and Arab philosophers of their garb; we have had them translated by chosen men, maintaining faithfully the virginity of the words. We do not wish to keep them all to ourselves; you are the first to whom we send them, since you are the nurslings of philosophy who shall draw water out of old cisterns. Do you make them public for the use of your students, to the glory of your Caesar."

I include here all that comes under the heading of natural philosophy and the more specialized studies of nature. I do this not to create a new class of true philosophers, which is neither useful nor possible in any event. I do this to expand our common knowledge of the natural world so that it might be put to better use to secure human ends.

Master Theodore: You have taken this approach in your book on falcons.

Frederick II: Yes, It is important to see all that exists, as it actually exists, and not to speculate vainly in fanciful ways. In this fashion we are likely to learn many things which are of use to the well-being of our kingdom. I oppose the practices of those rulers and church leaders who prohibit, or even burn, the works of Aristotle, or Averroes or other thoughtful men. When Paris decided in 1210 to burn the works of Aristotle and others, I made very clear that these thinkers were still freely available in my kingdom. No man or no kingdom will be improved by forbidding the use of reason. It is through reason—to see things as they actually are—that both true contemplation and the useful ends of knowledge can be achieved.

On the Sun

Master Theodore: You speak often of reason and knowledge, words which seem to have many meanings. What do you mean by knowledge and how are we to obtain it?

The Ascent

Frederick II: Let us begin with Plato, who has been so influential in shaping the thinking of the west. He speaks of philosophers, who one supposes to be wiser than the mass of men and who are therefore to be compelled to rule over just cities. These are the ones, he has Socrates say, who rise above that which merely comes into and goes out of being. They make the difficult ascent to knowledge of what is real, that is, what is eternal. But has Plato spoken honestly?

Master Theodore: Explain your meaning.

Frederick II: First, we should ask why obtaining knowledge is considered an ascent. What has knowledge to do with the spatial term of ascent, or going up? After all, Plato says the Ideas of which there can be genuine intellection are not to be found in space at all, and even if they are patterns or models for the world of becoming, they remain pure and separate from those images which are said to "participate" in them. They do not enter the sensible world of becoming but remain aloof as a pattern.

Master Theodore: What does it mean to "participate" in the Ideas?

Frederick II: It must mean to resemble or be similar in some fashion to the Ideas. Anything else, as Aristotle says, would be meaningless.

Master Theodore: The Ideas then remain separate from images of them.

Frederick II: When an image is said to participate in an Idea it takes nothing away from the Idea, which remains as it is. And as Ideas are nowhere to be found in space, we must not take the idea of ascent to be the truth, but only a figure. Even in the sensible world of becoming which Plato describes in *Timaeus,* he says the cosmos is a sphere about which, properly speaking, it is not possible to speak of what is up or down, left or right.

Master Theodore: Why this figure of ascent, which we find not only in *Timaeus* but also in the *Republic* which many commentators have described to us? We see this figure in the three monotheisms as well.

Frederick II: Yes. Among the Jews god seems to reside somewhere above us, in a heavenly abode of some sort. Moses must go up the mountain of Sinai to speak with god and receive his commands for the Jews. Among Christians we see that god's son Jesus comes down to the earth and then ascends to heaven which is celebrated by the church as Ascension Day. We see this too in Islam, where Muhammad goes up to a cave in the hills to receive the words given to him by the spirit Gabriel.

Master Theodore: What is the reason these faiths say that we must ascend in order to know god? Do they follow Plato in this?

Frederick II: There are similarities between these faiths and Plato, which we will explore. But they do not follow Plato in this. Men seem always to have regarded what is higher to be superior to what is lower; indeed these words are often used to mean the same thing. We see this in the thrones of kings which are elevated above all others. We see this in the language of all peoples, who say their authorities rule "over" them. We see this in the construction of castles and citadels and in military formations where it is always preferable to be above attackers. People seem always to have looked up to the sky to find their gods. This is true for those who worship the sun and for the three monotheistic faiths as well.

Master Theodore: Plato follows this common convention.

Frederick II: Yes, his story in *Timaeus* seems quite similar to the beliefs of the ancient Egyptians, from whom some say it is derived. He offers it as a "probable account" which cannot be more than probable as it concerns the sensible world of becoming, of which for Plato nothing can be known with certainty. He embellishes his story in many ways, including his amusing account of human anatomy. The gods placed the human head, which is the locus of intellect, atop a body which is erect, so that human souls would not be so undignified as to roll about the world.

Master Theodore: Philosophers do not suppose that gods or Ideas are to be found in places which are either above or below, or in any other location in space.

Frederick II: Philosophers say that gods or Ideas are found nowhere and everywhere, without any location in space. Maimonides, for example, says "we must not suppose that the Supreme Being occupies a place to which we can ascend, or from which we can descend." Plato speaks more honestly when he says men do not obtain knowledge through an ascent, but from a kind of turning around, though this too is a figure. It speaks of turning away from the sensible world of bodily desires to seek wisdom.

Master Theodore: This figure is also found in the monotheistic faiths, each of which speaks of turning away from the desires of the body and toward god. But however this is described—whether as an ascent or as a turning around—what is it that men can come to know from this process?

Frederick II: For Plato it means to approach intellection of the Ideas which are the patterns for all that exists in the sensible world. For the monotheistic faiths it means to approach god.

Master Theodore: In what does such knowledge actually consist?

Frederick II: Plato says the Ideas are the proper objects of our intellection. But what this means is harder to say. It cannot involve what we call discursive reason. Knowledge of the Ideas cannot come in the form of a definition using other words, or as an axiom, a deduction, a hypothesis, or an observation based upon our senses. They are in this way beyond our normal use of reason in which we define one thing in terms of another, but are found through what Plato calls a kind of mental seeing or an intellection. As the name implies in the Greek language, the Ideas are perhaps better said to be "seen" than known through discursive reason. They are to be apprehended through a kind of mental seeing analogous to our sight in the sensible world.

Master Theodore: Can you clarify with an example?

Frederick II: Let us take the notion of justice, about which we have previously spoken. There are many actions which we commonly call just or unjust. What do we mean when we say this? There must be a model of justice—what Plato calls an Idea—by which we understand the justness of any action. This Idea of justice is that which we can somehow know—or see, on the analogy of sight—by which to guide our practice. Socrates says we "glimpse" Ideas like this.

Master Theodore: With all due respect, let me press you further on this. Let us say that we know or see or glimpse the Idea of justice. What does this actually mean? This seems unable to be said, except upon the analogy of sight. It is sometimes said that Socrates must speak with analogies because he is conversing with men who are not philosophers. But what would he say differently if he were speaking to a philosopher like himself? Why does Socrates say that such a mental seeing is possible? And even if the Idea of justice can be seen or known in some way, could it be communicated to others?

Frederick II: Interesting questions, Master Theodore. Plato nowhere says that there must be such Ideas because he has known or seen them, choose what word you will, in such a fashion they can be communicated directly to others. He says there must be Ideas because if there were not, there would be no difference between opinion and knowledge, even if the opinion is somehow true opinion.

Master Theodore: The Ideas are necessary because there is, or somehow must be, a difference between knowledge and opinion?

Frederick II: Yes, he offers a kind of syllogism. Calcidius, the great translator and commentator on *Timaeus* says this: "All ... hold it as certain that there are in us the senses and also intellect, and that they are not the same as one another; and consequently that since they are themselves different in kind their effects, those of the senses and of intelligence, are different as well. And given that this is so, it is necessary also that there should be objects of which there are thoughts as also those of which there are sense perceptions." Plato always begins his investigation of Ideas by first considering the world of opinions and from this aims to discover Ideas.

Master Theodore: Is there a path which can take us to knowledge of or to the sight of Ideas?

Frederick II: Plato has Socrates propose just such a course of study. Socrates proposes music and gymnastics, then mathematics and astronomy—though the latter to be learned with an eye to what is permanent—and then at last dialectic, which is his own characteristic way of investigation.

Master Theodore: Will this necessarily produce knowledge of the Ideas, or even philosophers who aspire to such knowledge?

Frederick II: By no means. This education may produce better men, but philosophers are very rare. We might say that no philosopher, including Socrates himself, was ever educated in this way.

Master Theodore: There is then no assured path to intellection of the Ideas?

Frederick II: It is said by commentators that Plato offers two paths to intellection of the Ideas. One is what might be called the path of negation or dialectic. This is the path which Parmenides pursued. In displaying the limited and often self-contradictory opinions about justice, a philosopher moves closer to what is truly the Idea of justice.

Master Theodore: This is much the same as the path of the so-called negative theologians. They seek out the many things which god is not in order to come closer to an idea of what god is. But it seems in both cases this process demonstrates what is not, but never arrives at its goal—what the Ideas or the gods are.

Frederick II: This is fair to say, Master Theodore. Plato also proposes a second path which is that of analogy, which I have already mentioned. In saying that intellection is analogous to seeing—which we all experience—he hopes to clarify what is meant by knowing.

Master Theodore: But we must assume this analogy is well-founded.

Frederick II: That too is fair to say. But it is also true that it is perhaps impossible to describe what is invisible except upon some analogy to what is visible.

Master Theodore: Do Plato's Ideas cause the sensible world of becoming to exist?

Frederick II: The Ideas are not the efficient cause of the sensible world, which must be explained in a different way. The sensible world resembles the Ideas upon which it is patterned but it is not created by these Ideas. Rather, one might say that the Ideas cause the "whatness" of the sensible world which we observe, that is, they enable us to understand it, if imperfectly.

Master Theodore: What causes the Ideas to exist?

Frederick II: Here Plato speaks only in figures. He says that both light and vision are needed to see, but by themselves are not sufficient. For this we also need the sun, which is the source of light. In such a way are we to understand knowledge. Both intellection and the Ideas—which are intelligible—are needed to achieve knowledge but they themselves are not sufficient. What enables knowledge must be beyond both intellection and the Ideas and which allows them to be yoked together. This Plato calls in the *Republic* the Idea of the good. This is the enabling power behind the possibility of knowledge.

Master Theodore: As hard as it is to know the Ideas, it must be harder yet for men to form any conception of the Idea of the good.

Frederick II: Socrates never says that men can know the Idea of the good, at least in any way in which it can be described or communicated. Of what could such knowledge consist? It cannot be defined in terms of anything else; it allows what is intelligible to be known, but it is itself beyond being and therefore not intelligible. It is perhaps not proper to speak of knowing the Idea of the good; perhaps it is better to say it might somehow be glimpsed or experienced in a mystical kind of way, as some of Plato's successors have suggested. Macrobius says: "Thus Plato, when he was of a mind to talk about the good, did not dare to say what it is, since the only thing he knew about it was that it cannot be known by men." Plato is said here to follow the ancient Egyptian view concerning the first of all principles, which Damascius says they regarded as a "thrice unknown darkness."

Master Theodore: Such a thing could surely not be communicated to others.

Frederick II: Proclus says: "For it is not possible to apprehend it [the Idea of the good] intellectually, because it is unknown, nor to unfold it, because it is uncircumscribed; but whatever you may say of it, you will speak of a *certain thing* and you will speak *about* it, but you will not speak it. For speaking of the things of which it is the cause, we are unable to apprehend through intelligence *what it is*." What makes intelligibility possible is not itself intelligible or able to be communicated. Plato says in his 7th letter that the intellection of an Idea comes "of a sudden" and that is why his doctrine is neither written down nor ever will be.

Master Theodore: This is very much like the philosophical theologians' view of god. We must seek knowledge of god in the limited way human reason can proceed. We can do so by negations and analogies, but never directly. God is far beyond direct human comprehension. Our way of comprehension is not like god's; he may comprehend things directly but we can know things only in terms of one another.

Frederick II: This is well said, Master Theodore, and hints at the limits of human reason which we will discuss in due course.

Master Theodore: How then does Plato's sensible world of becoming come into existence if the Ideas do not create it?

Frederick II: It comes into existence by the work of what Timaeus calls a "craftsman" or a "father," which others have also called a fabricator, an artificer or a demiurge. Timeaus says, however, that "this maker and father of the universe is a hard task to find, and having found him it would be impossible to declare him to all mankind."

Master Theodore: Many among the three monotheistic faiths have identified this craftsman with their idea of god.

Frederick II: It is easy to see why. Like the three monotheistic gods, Plato's craftsman confronts a void or chaos which he makes good by bringing order to it. But there are differences. Plato's craftsman does not create the cosmos from nothing. He models it after a pattern which exists eternally. He is not responsible for creating this pattern, as nothing which is eternal is ever created. Nor of course

143

is he responsible for the Idea of the good. Plato has no concern to demonstrate that prior to the sensible world there was nothing but a void from which his craftsman created the world *ex nihilo.*

Master Theodore: Was this craftsman free to create a different world?

Frederick II: Timaeus almost speaks as if that were possible, that his craftsman might not have chosen to model the sensible world after the pattern of the eternal Ideas. But it seems upon reflection he never would wish to create anything less than what is best; therefore of course he chose to create the world he did.

Master Theodore: Are there other differences?

Frederick II: The gods of the three monotheistic faiths seem to have more power than Plato's craftsman, whose sole purpose is to make the existing void or chaos orderly and therefore good. The monotheistic gods are like Plato's craftsman in that they are not subject to death or corruption; but unlike Plato's craftsman they do not confront a pre-existing set of Ideas including the Idea of the good, which are eternal. Philo, who as always aims to reconcile Hebrew scripture with Plato, suggests there was a "double creation," first as an idea in god's mind and then with material bodies, complete with men and women.

The monotheistic gods seem freer to create the world, and also to destroy it, as they please, and nowhere is it said they are working after a pattern which is eternal. They are described as omnipotent. They can and do intervene in the world which they have created. Plato's craftsman seems to have one task only, and he delegates any future involvement in the cosmos to the lesser gods who are called his "sons."

Master Theodore: As we have discussed, the three monotheistic faiths struggle with the question of how an omnipotent god could create a world with evil in it. They sometimes conclude that their god was not entirely free to create as he pleased, but faced some limits. They say ours is not a perfect world, but the best possible world. This is a kind of limit upon god.

Frederick II: Yes, as we have discussed, it is a difficult problem to reconcile god's omnipotence with a less than perfect world. The only solution available is to say that what appears to us imperfect is not so for god. This question seems at first to be less of a problem for Plato. Plato's Timaeus says that his craftsman modeled the sensible world after the pattern of the Ideas, but that he also required something into which to pour, as it were, the sensible world he created. This he refers to as a kind of receptacle, which some have likened to space and others to matter or substance. This he also refers to as a kind of "necessity" with which his craftsman must work. This necessity limits the perfect freedom of his craftsman; Plato says the craftsman must "persuade" necessity so as to allow order to come into the motionless void which has not yet been ensouled.

Master Theodore: Souls, which move what exists in the sensible world, also pre-existed this world?

Frederick II: Yes, souls are said to pre-exist the sensible world and also to be immortal.

Master Theodore: What can we know of this receptacle into which the ensouled world is poured?

Frederick II: It is said to have no qualities of its own, so it cannot be air, water, fire or earth, as earlier thinkers had proposed. It has no qualities of its own, but is purely empty potential.

Master Theodore: Can such a thing be comprehended?

Frederick iI: Plato says it can be comprehended only by a kind of bastard or illegitimate reasoning, by which he seems to mean an inference. It is situated between being and non-being and thus is not able to be comprehended in the same way as being, but only in a mysterious way.

Master Theodore: Unless this receptacle, this necessity has some potential to be patterned after the Ideas in various ways, would not the sensible world all be one and the same, with none of the diversity we know it to have?

Frederick II: Yes, that seems to be quite true. Proclus makes just this point in the 142nd proposition of his *Elements of Theology*. In the end Plato struggles with just the same question as do the three monotheistic faiths, that is, why what exists, exists just as it does and not otherwise. About this there is only speculation.

Master Theodore: Plato then supposes a set of eternal Ideas, including the Idea of the good, a divine craftsman, and the motionless void of necessity—all of which are required to bring into existence the sensible world. And as they are eternal and uncreated, they cannot be said to have any purpose.

Frederick II: This is true. As we have discussed, only that which is created can be said to have a purpose. The purpose of Plato's craftsman is to share the goodness of the eternal patterns, which he wished to copy. In the beautiful phrase of Proclus, this reflected the "exuberant plenitude" of the craftsman. But as to the Ideas, the receptacle or the craftsman himself, what purpose could be ascribed to them?

Master Theodore: Is Plato's craftsman to be understood as he is presented, namely, as having human characteristics such as choosing, sharing and creating? Is the craftsman a kind of superhuman god?

Frederick II: Here we must attend carefully to what Plato says, as he often speaks in figures. One might better suppose that his craftsman is will itself, which he personifies to make it easier to understand. It is intellect which then brings order out of chaos, and it can do so only because the Ideas—which are intelligible—exist as patterns. If the Ideas did not exist intellect would be unable to find order in chaos. In this way order is brought to the world by intellect, which without Ideas would be as little possible as sight without light.

But this does not explain the existence of the sensible world. We might say that for Plato all that exists has no discernible purpose, but it is at least partially knowable.

Master Theodore: It seems that each of the creation accounts of the sensible world requires an invisible power which lies behind it. This might be called a craftsman, or intellect, or the One of Plotinus or the gods of the three monotheistic faiths.

Frederick II: This is well said, Master Theodore. This is a deep reflection about our thinking, namely, that the visible world must be understood in terms of what is invisible, which makes what is visible possible. Philosophers and theologians have learned this deep truth as a result of what is called in a figure their ascent.

The Descent

Master Theodore: Do philosophers—or prophets, as some are called—come back to the visible world better suited to live or to rule in this world? Of what practical use is knowledge of invisible, immaterial and unchanging Ideas and forces?

Frederick II: You are asking what philosophers have learned that they may bring back with them on their return to the sensible world in which we live.

Master Theodore: Yes, exactly.

Frederick II: The Ideas, including the Idea of the good, remain apart from the sensible world. They cannot be brought down, so to say, to perfect the sensible world, nor can the gods of the three monotheistic faiths be brought down. In Plato's case one may say there is no instruction or guidance to be found in the Idea of the good. It can barely be comprehended in any way, save to serve as a necessity to yoke the intellect with what is intelligible. It provides no standards for the organization of the sensible world. It is a majestic vision, not a source of rules.

Master Theodore: Plato is said to draw an image of this in the *Republic.*

Frederick II: Yes, commentators tell us that he speaks of a philosopher who ascends from the shadows of a cave to see objects in the light of the sun. He sees more clearly than do those who remain in the cave. When he returns to the cave, however, he is not greeted warmly by those who have remained there. What he has seen is said by those in the cave to be ridiculous and is not credited. In fact, his own vision when he returns to the cave is blurry as well.

Master Theodore: Plato says the men in the cave are not able to recognize the blessings which the philosopher could deliver to them.

Frederick II: Yes, he blames the people living in the shadows for their inability to understand and to accept what the philosopher has seen. But is this true? What useful knowledge has the philosopher who has contemplated the Ideas, and especially the Idea of the good, to share with mankind? Let us take as an example the Idea of justice. Socrates demonstrates the limitations of all conventional notions of justice, suggesting they all fall short in some way. But he is unable to speak the Idea of justice or to offer a definition of justice, much less to say how it can be applied in the actual practice of ruling. He seems to have learned nothing at all which can be communicated about how justice can be approximated in the sensible world. At best he has suggested only that a life dedicated to the search for justice, as was his own life, is somehow more just and also more pleasurable.

But how does this assist those who rule in the sensible world, as I do? It seems that only Plato's craftsman, the god who brought order to the sensible world, can in any way pattern the sensible world after the Ideas. The philosophers who descend, if I may use that word, to the cities of the sensible world have little to offer to actual rulers. One who has glimpsed the Idea of the good, and therefore too the other Ideas including justice, is as ignorant about how to rule as anyone else. Though the men chained in the cave do not appreciate the beauty and joy of seeing clearly, that is, what is called divine contemplation, they are not entirely wrong about the philosopher's use to their lives. The philosopher comes back to the cave a changed man, but he is also empty-handed. The Ideas remain accessible to intellect but cannot be transferred in their pure form to the sensible world. A ruler who must confront the actual problems of governance in the sensible world will find a philosopher to be of little use. With all respect, that is why I philosophize with you, but do not consult you about our laws or my military campaigns.

Master Theodore: Could one say the same for those monotheistic thinkers who investigate their gods in a philosophic way, that is, with reason?

Frederick II: Yes, very much so. Philosophers who seek the gods of the three monotheistic faiths through reason bring very little wisdom to the world of practice. We have discussed several times already the way of negative theology. As we have said, this tells us what god is not, but does not tell us what god is. Surely the wise Maimonides must have understood this limitation when he says negative theology is the way to god. How could he know this, if his goal remains elusive? He hints at this difficulty when he says it is difficult to form an idea of either the actions of incorporeal beings or the beings themselves. This path leads to what is imponderable, that of which we can form no mental picture at all. This is spoken of in the *Liber de causis* which some have attributed to Aristotle. It says there that the first cause—which men have often called by the name of god—is above all knowledge and description. It is that which must be assumed but not that of which we can have genuine knowledge.

Master Theodore: This extends even to god's name.

Frederick II: Yes, the 166th proposition of this book says "The first cause is above any name by which it is named." We see this same thought expressed most beautifully by the Pythagorean philosopher Sextus who says "Do not investigate the name of god because you will not find it. For every thing which is called by a name, receives its appellation from that which is more worthy than itself … Who is it, therefore, who has given a name to god? God, however, is not a name to God, but an indication of what we conceive of him."

Master Theodore: Men always fail to capture the name of god, for he has no name. If men could properly name god, this would make them superior to god.

Frederick II: Just so. Moses learned this in a rather direct manner. In speaking with god, he seeks god's name. God tells him only this, which we say in Latin: *"Ego sum qui sum"* (I am who I am).

Master Theodore: The prophets of the three monotheistic faiths claim they are able to say more than this about their gods.

Frederick II: Yes, but what they say is not derived from reason. Rather it is based upon a claim that god has somehow spoken directly to them, which others must believe in order to credit their descriptions of god. I remind you that in each case these claims are not based upon seeing god but upon hearing from god.

Master Theodore: Does not Hebrew scripture say that Moses beheld the likeness of god and that he spoke to god "mouth to mouth?"

Frederick II: Maimonides explains this. He says Moses did not actually see god, because god cannot be seen; it means that his meetings with god were direct and not mediated by, say, an angel.

Master Theodore: Even those who claim to have heard directly from god usually say far less about the nature of their god than about what their god commands men to do.

Frederick II: Yes, we see this with Moses who receives what he purports to be the commands of god.

Master Theodore: Moses then descends to the sensible world to bring the commands of god to men.

Frederick II: Yes, and like the philosopher of Plato's cave, he is not well-received. In his absence the Jews have turned to worship a golden idol. To impress his views upon the people, he smashes the commands of god and returns to receive a new set of commands. But he must also take the practical step of slaughtering many thousands of Jews who oppose him. Only then are his commands accepted.

Master Theodore: Christianity takes a different course, but comes more or less to the same place.

Frederick II: Jesus is said not to be a prophet of god but part of god himself. He is said to be a son of god, who is his father. He provided a tangible, sensible form of god while he was on earth. This is a great difference between Christianity and Judaism and Islam. But Jesus was not well-received either, and it took several centuries and much bloodshed for Christianity to be accepted. But Jesus too said very little about what his father was like and Christians have had to infer much— such as that god is a god of love and that Jesus was god's only-begotten son—from the words which Jesus spoke while he was on earth. Jesus spoke far more about the kind of life which men should live than about the nature of god. Nor did Jesus descend to earth with counsel that is useful for those who rule; as we have discussed, he suggests that those who rule do so with god's permission, else they would not rule at all.

Master Theodore: Speak too of Muhammad.

Frederick II: Like Moses, Muhammad claims to have heard directly from god, in his case through god's messenger the spirit Gabriel. But he too speaks far more about god's commands and punishments than about the nature of god. And as he makes clear in many places in the Qu'ran his message was not well-received at first either, and had to be cemented by a series of military battles against those who disbelieved his claims.

Master Theodore: Unlike Plato's philosopher these men bring concrete and specific commands for how men are to live.

Frederick II: Yes. This is the important part of their work. They do not teach contemplation of god in order to come closer to him, but a set of commands which men are to follow. The way to please god is not to know his essence, but to follow his commands. Prophets are able to speak in this way not because they have seen or reasoned their way to god but because they have heard what god has spoken either directly or through a messenger. But it must be added that even the claims of prophets apparently fall short of providing complete and unambiguous guidance, and hence we have seen both extensive and wildly divergent interpretations of the words of god and many disagreements within each monotheistic faith about how men are to live.

Master Theodore: Though each faith speaks mostly about the commands of its god, prophets seem still to say at least something about their gods.

Frederick II: That is fair to say. That god favors the Jews, or that god gave his son to be sacrificed or that god demands obedience on the threat of eternal damnation—these are all things which are said to be spoken by god.

Master Theodore: It seems that a philosophy such as Plato's or that of religious sages, unlike the prophets, offers very little counsel for those who rule in this world.

Frederick II: Plato does not represent whatever he has learned as coming directly from the voice of god. He aims always to learn what he can by reason and presents his account of the gods as "probable" and lacking clear commands for men. But there is one way in which Plato believes that what he calls an ascent to knowledge can lead a philosopher to be a better ruler. It is not that a philosopher gains specific knowledge about how to govern that is unavailable to others; it is because his love of wisdom—the search for the first causes of all that is—moderates his bodily and worldly desires. A philosopher is less moved than other men by love of money, fame or power. If one with a philosophic temper should rule, he will do so freer of the desire to use his power to achieve his own private ends; he will be freer to look after the common good of those over whom he rules. Plato has Socrates say that if one comes to know something after his arguments, he will be better off; but even if one does not learn what he seeks, he will be gentler and less harsh. This is the virtue of dialectic.

Master Theodore: This is to say he will not be inclined to rule as a tyrant might rule.

Frederick II: There is another long syllogism at work here. Love of wisdom leads to a search for the Ideas including the Idea of the good, which moderates desires of the body, which leads to greater care for the common good. All this is rather more asserted than demonstrated. I have found that it is quite possible to love both the things of this world and the search for wisdom. But Plato does make a plausible argument that if there were no such thing as the love of wisdom, tyranny would be a reasonable alternative.

Master Theodore: What does this say about our popes, who we must assume are men who love god?

Frederick II: Popes who earnestly seek knowledge of god, after the manner of philosophers or religious sages, might reasonably be expected to be good leaders of the church. But this is exactly the problem with the church today. Our popes assert their love to know god, and may even believe their own assertions. But these days popes are filled up with worldly desires—for riches, for fame and above all for power. That is why I have urged the leaders of the church to return to their simpler, less worldly origins. Today's popes are more temporal rulers than genuine seekers of god.

Master Theodore: Do Plato's philosophers have any other virtues which suit them to rule over men?

Frederick II: Much practical experience is required to rule well. When he is at his most practical, as in his book called *The Laws,* Plato requires those who would rule in his well-governed city to have practical experience. He proposes a period of ten years before even the best of men are trusted with complete power. This serves not only to acquaint his philosophers with practical experience, but also ages them, which itself often has a moderating effect on men's worldly desires. I say "often," not always, as some of our aged popes—and I think especially of Gregory—seem not to have moderated their behavior in any noticeable way.

Master Theodore: This is certainly true, though with all respect I might say the popes see you in somewhat the same way.

Frederick II: Fair enough, Master Theodore. I take no offense.

Master Theodore: You have pursued philosophic studies yourself.

Frederick II: Philosophy is a most pleasurable enterprise. It is an enterprise for which one always wishes to have fewer responsibilities and more leisure to pursue. I greatly enjoy my conversations with philosophers and religious sages of each of the three monotheistic faiths. I have conversed with wise men from many parts of the world and men who hold many different opinions. But I have also conversed with many philosophers who would make terrible rulers, so little is the connection between love of wisdom concerning first causes and the demands of leadership. I am of the mind that what I learn from my philosophical conversations is a very great joy, but I do not for that reason find much that is of practical use for governing.

Master Theodore: What then shall we conclude about the so-called ascent to the world of Ideas and the descent back to the sensible world?

Frederick II: We find that god, or the one, or the Idea of the good, or the first cause lies beyond all earthly things and beyond our human capacity to know clearly. Yet the so-called ascent to learn of the invisible entities which create and make knowable this world is where human joy and completeness are to be found. It appears that these invisible entities, call them what you may, seem—oddly, in a way—unable to rest within themselves but are somehow moved to create the great diversity of our constantly changing sensible world. As we aim to know about god, god for his part seems to come down to the sensible world. What then can we learn from reason? We can experience the joy of seeking the invisible entities and forces which create the world, but this knowledge, imperfect as it is, does not then come down to guide us in the sensible world. Only a god of the monotheistic faiths or the Timaean craftsman has the fulsome power to move out of itself and create the sensible world. We are left with a choice. Either we can attempt to scale the heights of wisdom to try to know god directly—which is never fully successful—or we can seek to learn about the sensible world which god has created and which therefore can teach us by inference something about that god.

Master Theodore: Can we not do both?

Frederick II: Yes, of course. But here is my point: we should not expect to learn the same kinds of things from both paths. There is no single path that takes us directly up and down. We cannot expect to travel these paths in the way that a god could travel them, but only in ways which teach us different things. In the end we come back to where we started.

We can perhaps gain a hint about god from contemplating the invisible forces which created and impel the world. Such speculation, however, will not teach us much about how the visible world works, that is, how the first cause created the world in just such a way that its secondary causes operate. To gain the latter kind of knowledge we must study the visible world. To my mind—despite the opaque saying of Heracleitus—the way up and the way down are not at all the same.

Master Theodore: The claims of prophets are based upon what they say is direct revelation from god rather than what we can learn from reason, either in an ascent to first causes or through a study of the sensible world.

Frederick II: We cannot hope to gain knowledge of the sensible world by way of an ascent to what is first, be it called god, the one, the Idea of the good or the first cause. Only those who claim to have heard the words of god directly—prophets—make such claims. They claim to have found a short path which is unknown to men generally, to learn how we should live in the visible world. But these claims are many and contradictory, which would be surprising for a god to have given to men. It would also be surprising to see such a wide divergence of views if each prophet truly heard directly from god.

Master Theodore: Reason will not tell us very much about the first causes. The claims of prophets extend far beyond where reason can take us and will lead in many directions depending upon the prophets themselves. Is there an irreducible minimum upon which all three monotheistic faiths can agree that reason can teach us about god?

The Visible and the Invisible

Frederick II: When they are most honest, philosophers and religious sages say very little about god and his qualities. They take non-predication of god very far. They do not wish to limit god by human qualities. But some aim to deduce the qualities of god from their definitions of god. Most of these are not to be credited. Most are simply inferences which are drawn from what men admire. That god is one or three or many; that god is loving or merciful; that god is omnipotent or omniscient; or that god acts always with reason—these claims can be asserted but never demonstrated. Each rests upon the notion that god can be described according to what men value most highly.

Master Theodore: This leads to a very empty idea of god. Is there no quality of god which can be known by reason, a quality without which the idea of god would not meaningfully exist?

Frederick II: There is one such quality and upon this the three monotheistic faiths, as well as Plato, are in agreement. One can think away many of the human qualities attributed to god and a god might still exist. One can think away the notions of god having a voice or sight or any other sense. Muslim theologians have long debated this question. The Mutazilites say that god cannot "see" as we do, because this would be to give god eyes. The Asharites make the strange claim that god can have vision without a body. But there is one quality attributed to god which cannot be thought away without making the meaning of god disappear as well. This is the notion of power or force or what is often called "will."

Master Theodore: Is not will a human quality derived from our own experience, and in this way like other human qualities which men have given to god?

Frederick II: Yes, but the idea of god's power or force or will is the necessary human attribute for faith. Without god's will no world is created or sustained. Without god's will there is no meaning to the idea of god's commands to men or the requirement of obedience to god. One may say that god does not will by "speaking" or in other humanly understandable ways; but the power or force behind these words must always be assumed, and that capacity is most often known by what we call "will." Whether god speaks or thinks the world into existence, god is somehow wiling it. All creation, even if it differs from human creating, is an act of will. For this reason many thinkers of the monotheistic faiths have identified god's essence with his will.

Master Theodore: Might we not say, as some have, that god creates not through an act of will but simply from an overflowing of his bounty?

Frederick II: Would you then say that god wills despite himself, that he has no intent to create the world but that it simply happens to him or through him? This is very far from the view of the three monotheistic faiths which see the world as a definite act of god's will. And for that matter, it differs from Plato's account in *Timaeus* as well. His craftsman may have wished to model the world after the eternal Ideas out of a bountiful love, but he nevertheless had to will in order to achieve this. No less an interpreter than Proclus says that Plato's demiurge creates through an act of will.

Master Theodore: Might one not say that god does not stand outside the world but is a pre-condition of the possibility of the world itself? That is, that the world just *is*, and god is the word we use to say this?

Frederick II: This is what is said by David of Dinant. Our great Albert, as I learned, is very critical of David of Dinant's writing. For David of Dinant the world is god made perceptible. David says "the form that comes to matter is nothing other than God making himself into what is perceptible." This we call by the name pantheism. And it is well to remember that his views were declared heretical by the church and his works, along with those of Aristotle and Averroes, were ordered to be burned at Paris in 1210. As I have said, I of course urged scholars at my university to ignore such bans.

Master Theodore: One could read Plato's *Timaeus* in this way as well, that the sensible world is god made perceptible.

Frederick II: This is so.

Master Theodore: The three monotheistic faiths all speak of god's will or power to create, to order and to reorder the world.

Frederick II: As the three monotheistic faiths unfold one after another in time, each seems to stress the will of god more and more fully. For the Jews god creates the world and acts within it on behalf of one people. For Christians god created the world in the manner said by the Torah and continues to act among all peoples through the power of the holy spirit. Augustine says in his *Confessions* that the will of god belongs to his very substance. And for the Muslims above all others, god's will is most central. Avicenna, for example, says that god does not have a will, but is will itself. In this way the sensible world and all that is in being is radically contingent—unconnected to our human understanding of good and of reason—and fully dependent from moment to moment on the will of god.

Master Theodore: How do you understand the meaning of the word to "will?"

Frederick II: It can be described as a self-moving impulse, as energy or as a force which creates change or motion in the sensible world. It is what is meant by the Greek word *dunamis.* It is of course modeled on our experience of human will, which we understand intuitively.

Master Theodore: Men do not perhaps will as fully as god, but they do will.

Frederick II: This is surely the view of the Jews, Christians and many Muslims. Some Muslim thinkers, however, believe that god's will is not simply the most powerful of wills, but is the only will that exists. For them human free will is an illusion that accompanies our actions which are in fact determined by god. Others suggest that god has "loaned" some of his will to men, but that he might take it back at any moment.

Master Theodore: As we have discussed, the notion of will seems to require reason to accompany it, if there is to be any choice about what is willed.

Frederick II: Yes, an idea of will which is modeled on human will must have this character. What is willed must somehow be chosen, that is, there must be a chance the will might have chosen differently. But if one takes the notion of will as impulse or force or power, there may or may not be choice involved, but rather necessity.

Master Theodore: In either case there must be some impulse for what is self-moving, whether we see this as freely chosen or as necessary.

Frederick II: Just so. Human wills are said to be driven by the impulse which has been called *eros* or desire. This is a lack, a want, a privation, and so cannot be said of god who is supposed to be self-sufficient, that is, to lack nothing outside himself. It is more difficult, as we will discuss, to describe what is the impulse to an action which is thought to be necessary. It must be a kind of internal power which we do not fully understand.

Master Theodore: Human beings will in time.

Frederick II: Yes, but this too cannot be said of a god who is outside of time, which he has created in the very act of willing the sensible world to exit.

Master Theodore: Are the words for human will and god's will then at all comparable?

Frederick II: The idea of willing, in the sense we understand human willing, cannot occur without desire and cannot occur outside of time. Such a notion is a meaningless sequence of words. But without a notion like this—of capacity, of power, of self-movement— how can it be imagined that god has created the world?

Master Theodore: Humans are said to will because they are ensouled.

Frederick II: Yes, soul is the name of the self-movement of whatever exists, including human beings.

Master Theodore: Is god therefore ensouled?

Frederick II: This is a very difficult question, Master Theodore. If god's creation is thought to be willed in any way, this must be so. Whatever moves itself is ensouled; this is what it means to be ensouled. But if god's creation of the world is said somehow not to require movement on the part of god, perhaps it need not be said that god is ensouled. But will without self-movement is impossible to understand and is meaningless. Plato speaks of this in *Timaeus* when he says the craftsman ensouled the entire cosmos which moves itself in the fashion of a world-animal. Soul, he says, is woven throughout the cosmos and is the self-motion of the planets, the stars, the earth, men, animals and plants. Some have said that soul causes this motion, but perhaps it is better said that soul is the name to describe beings with self-motion. Plato never addresses whether his craftsman is ensouled, but we must suppose that this is so.

Master Theodore: Whether we speak of the creations of the gods or of what is ensouled self-movement in the sensible world, it seems that the forces which move—whether they are described as will or as blind power or force—have a common characteristic: they are all invisible.

Frederick II: Yes, what is invisible creates what comes to be visible. It creates what we can perceive by seeing or hearing or by means of our other senses.

Master Theodore: This is said by all three monotheistic faiths.

Frederick II: You will recall that Moses instructed the Jews not to worship what exists in the sensible world—especially the sun—but rather that invisible spiritual power which is god who is said to have created the sensible world. And you will find this in Christianity as well; Paul says in Romans 1:20: "Ever since the creation of the world his [god's] invisible nature, namely his eternal power and deity, have been clearly perceived in the things that have been made." And again Paul says in Colossians 1:15 that Jesus is the perceptible image of an invisible god. This was affirmed at both the Council of Nicaea in 325 and the Council at Constantinople in 381, which speak of god as the creator of all things "visible and invisible." And many suras in the Qu'ran say that anyone who has reason can see that the world, in all its order and splendor and fittedness for human life, has been created by a god which no man—including Muhammad—has ever seen. The Qu'ran pointedly warns man not to bow down and worship the sun.

Master Theodore: The idea that what is visible is created by what is invisible seems to pervade our thinking at every turn.

Frederick II: Aristotle says that the earliest natural philosophers were materialists, who saw the world only as matter in motion. They did not examine the idea of motion or how it is caused. Aristotle says that Anaxagoras was the first Greek philosopher to say that *mind*, which is invisible, is the cause of all that exists. And Anaxagoras was followed by Empedocles who saw the invisible forces of *eros* and *strife* as the causes of what occurs in the visible world. Pythagoras saw the visible world arising out of number, which is invisible.

Master Theodore: This is Plato's view as well.

Frederick II: Yes, in two ways. The Idea of the good, which as an idea is of course invisible, is the cause of our ability to know the "whatness" or as Proclus says the "essence" of things. And the invisible god who is Plato's craftsman is responsible for creating what order and movement there is by infusing the invisible power of soul into it. Soul is incorporeal, spiritual and invisible; it is not to be thought of as breath, for that would suggest that soul has a tangible, sensible quality which it does not.

Master Theodore: So whatever is the source of motion, leave aside the immensity of creation, is always invisible?

Frederick II: Yes, it seems so. Maimonides concludes, for example, that whatever goes from potential to actual requires a third force, which is itself invisible. Both what are called first causes and what are called secondary causes are invisible. An interpretation of Boethius' work on arithmetic by a very wise man of the recent past says this: "Physics is the recognition of the natures and hidden causes placed by God in things which, although they are not known by anyone, nevertheless it is possible to have the knowledge of practicing according to them."

Master Theodore: Why must we always seem to look behind what occurs, as it were, and seek invisible causes to explain the visible world? The earliest natural philosophers whom Aristotle mentions saw all of nature as alive, as self-moving, and so had no need to find external causes for this. The world simply was always in motion. This is how Philo describes the Chaldeans, as those who mistakenly believed only in causes they could see.

Frederick II: These natural philosophers were much like what later are called atomists. Atomists say that atoms have always been in motion, attracting and repelling and colliding with one another. No cause could be given for this; it is a world of chance and spontaneity.

Master Theodore: Why then do philosophers go behind this world and seek to explain it as a result of invisible forces?

Frederick II: A fair question, Master Theodore. The atomist view says that all that exists are atoms in motion. In thinking deeply, philosophers concluded that atomism, or materialism as it is sometimes called, is an insufficient and self-contradictory view of the world. To say there are only atoms in motion cannot be defended. After all, what are "atoms" and what is "motion?" These are not sensible realities lying at hand in nature. These are surely ideas. No atomist or materialist can do without ideas, from the first moment he tries to explain the sensible world. All of the philosophers, and especially Plato, are quite correct to say that ideas—which are invisible—exist. It cannot be otherwise without forfeiting the ability to speak about anything, including the theory of atomism.

And they are also quite correct to say there is something different about ideas than about what we sense. I have spoken about this at length with the great Leonardo of Pisa [who is known today as Fibonacci]. He, who has brought us the numerals by which the Arabs calculate, is the greatest mathematician in the world today. Consider the mathematical idea of equality. We might illustrate this by saying that if A=B and B=C, then A=C. We can suppose that any part of the sensible world, or even the entire sensible world might not exist. There is nothing to be faulted in that supposition. But we cannot suppose that in our example A does not equal C. This must be always and everywhere true. It is not contingent, that is, it does not come or go but abides forever.

Master Theodore: So ideas exist and are different from the impressions of sense.

Frederick II: That is quite correct. We might consider the following regarding the theory of atomism. There are atoms, which are understood by reason as an idea. But atomists do not explain how they know there are atoms. And there is motion, but atomists do not explain how they know it is motion, much less what motion is. What atoms are, that is to say, that they are comprehended as atoms at all, requires that they have a certain nature or character or form. It is reason, which employs ideas, to which we must give thanks to know that atoms have a certain form, that is, that they are to be understood at all apart from pure formlessness.

Pure formlessness may be called matter or a receptacle or substance, or any other name which you wish to give it. It may or may not be somehow differentiated in terms of its potential, as we have discussed. But to be understood in any way it must be given actuality by the forms which it assumes. What is this process of in-forming and from where does it come? These forms are known by intellection.

And so too with "motion," which is comprehended only by an idea, which in turn allows us to ask how motion comes to be at all. To account for these things philosophers seek a power, a force or an agency which causes them to be as our ideas have shown them to be. Perhaps nowhere is this premise of philosophic thought better spoken than at the very beginning of western thought by the ancient Pythagorean Archytas. He says in *On the Principles of Things*: "there are three principles; the subject of things (matter), form and that which is of itself motive, and invisible in power."

Illumination

Master Theodore: Let us accept then there are forces which are invisible. What can we know of them and how can we know this?

Frederick II: Let us suppose we are standing next to a rock. The sun is shining on both of us in the very same way. You might say that we are both illuminated by the same source. But we see both the sun and the rock, whereas—so far as we know—the rock sees neither us nor the sun. Why is this? Clearly the sun is necessary to our seeing; without it we would not see the rock. But more must be necessary than the sun. Men have the ability to respond to the illumination of the sun in a way the rock cannot.

Master Theodore: The stone responds by becoming warm.

Frederick II: Yes, just so. And we become warm as well. But men can also see the sun and the rock. Our ability to see contributes to what we see just as does the light of the sun.

Master Theodore: Your hunting falcons can see too.

Frederick II: Yes, their sight is far better than ours. Why then do we train them and they do not train us? The falcon can see its prey; it can distinguish it from, say, a tree or a rock. It can in this way see its prey

162

as prey. But we men have a far greater ability to see differences in the world, to name them, to see their "whatness," that is, to see them as they are. The sun is a necessary but by no means sufficient condition for seeing the "whatness" of what there is.

Master Theodore: Men do not simply perceive the sensible world, as if it impresses its qualities upon us without any contribution from us.

Frederick II: That is correct. There is a far closer connection between what we are said to perceive and knowledge than many philosophers suppose. When we perceive something as something, say a rock, this is not simply a perception but an intellection. What we call a rock—its combination of size, its weight and the hardness of its material –might well exist without our perception of it. But it would not exist as a "rock." If one of my hunting dogs—who have very keen perception—looks in the direction of my library shelves, what does he see? Perhaps he sees many colors and perhaps he can "see" that it is a barrier though which he cannot run. He certainly does not see it as a shelf of books. Maimonides correctly says of the human intellect that in comprehending a tree as a tree "the intellect is not a thing distinct from the thing comprehended … the thing comprehended is the abstract form of the tree, and at the same time is the intellect in action; and that the intellect and the abstract form of the tree are not two different things, for the intellect in action is nothing but the thing comprehended."

Master Theodore: What makes it possible to "see" such things as the books for what they are?

Frederick II: Plato says—and in this he is correct—we can see what we do because the ideas exist. If ideas—of rocks, or trees or books, for example—did not exist, we could not see these things for what they are. To see things for what they are is the beginning of all knowledge. This is the motto of my book on falcons: *manifestare ea quae sunt, sicut sunt* (to display the things that are, as they are). In this I follow Averroes.

Master Theodore: So far we have spoken of seeing things which are perceptible, such as rocks or books. How can we see what is invisible?

Frederick II: Here too we "see" because the ideas exist. There are ideas not only of what is visible but of what is invisible as well. Consider again our example of mathematical equality expressed as: if A=B and B=C, then A=C. To see this there must be available to us the idea of equality. Without it these letters and signs would be meaningless. Equality is not a feature lying at hand in the perceptible world, but is an idea. It is an idea which is invisible and which has no location in space. Even to know that A=B, leave aside the larger equation drawn from it, requires that there be an idea of equality. So too when we speak of beauty or justice or other incorporeal, non-sensible, invisible ideas.

But more needs to be said here. There are many ideas and many kinds of ideas. There is an idea of a tree and an idea of a circle. The idea of a circle allows of perfection, that is, it is a figure entirely equidistant from its center. We can judge how actual circles which are drawn are more or less close to a perfect circle. But consider the idea of a tree. There is no perfect idea of a tree. Is an olive tree or a shade tree closer to the perfect idea of a tree? Neither is so. What if the ideas of justice and beauty are like this? They do not admit of perfection or of judging closeness to an ideal, as does a circle or a square or a line. Plato misleads us here; he takes the mathematical idea of perfection and likens justice and beauty to them. We might see beauty in a woman or a painting or a vista of nature. Is any one of these somehow closer to perfect beauty? Each may be best in its own circumstance. Still, it is true that there is an idea of beauty which can be said of each, by which is meant what is most well-formed or pleasing.

Master Theodore: We say we "see" these ideas but do we really see them? Is this not a figure?

Frederick II: Knowing is indeed understood by analogy to seeing, but the relationship is far closer than you may think. As I have said, perception is only a part of what we call seeing, which is a disclosing of the "whatness" of things. That we "see" the truth is not far-fetched but is the core of what is meant by seeing at all.

Master Theodore: How do we have this capacity to know and to speak of these invisible ideas which our mind sees?

Frederick II: Men of faith say that god implants the ability in men to be illuminated in this way, which consists of both receiving illumination from the outside and converting it into seeing on the inside. Some, especially certain Muslim thinkers, say god is present on each and every occasion of such illumination. Others say god implanted within us the ability to be illuminated and that we now are illuminated on our own, as it were. Others have had the temerity to say that god is not involved at all, but that we simply have this ability from our nature.

Master Theodore: What is illuminated to us is a direct way of knowing. Mathematics is said to be the clearest example of this.

Frederick II: Yes, the formula A=B and B=C, therefore A=C constitutes a kind of direct knowing; one sees the truth of it immediately. All of mathematics is built upon the axioms we take as self-evident or indubitably known. But we must consider, as Plato has, that all of mathematics in turn rests upon simple ideas which are its foundation. We cannot speak of A=B without knowing the idea of equality. We cannot speak of the area of a triangle without knowing the ideas of triangle or area directly. We can examine these ideas but we will not learn much about them other than that they exist as they do. But they do exist, as they must if we are to have knowledge of anything at all.

Master Theodore: Ideas then certainly exist.

Frederick II: I am sometimes called by our popes a materialist, perhaps because of the sensual pleasures which I enjoy. But I am far from being a philosophical materialist, which is an obviously mistaken view of the world.

Master Theodore: Do we create these ideas ourselves?

Frederick II: To think this would be the opposite error of materialism. This would be to suggest that we humans have the ability to create the entire world, and ourselves within it, by ourselves. Our ideas do not create the world all by themselves. No ideas do. This would be like saying that we can have vision without light. The ideas we form play a role in knowing what is, but they do not create the world such as it is. We may apprehend the idea of anything we fancy. But this idea does not create the world as we know it. To think this would abolish the very possibility of any knowledge of what is.

Master Theodore: It seems you are saying that knowledge is a kind of revelation.

Frederick II: Yes, just so. Intellection of the ideas upon which our knowledge is based is a kind of illumination, a kind of immediate awareness of what is in front of us. As Plato says about his doctrine, "as a result of continued application and communion therewith, it is brought to birth in the soul of a sudden."

Master Theodore: It seems then that you are diminishing the distinction between reason and revelation which you described before.

Frederick II: All knowing is in the first instance a kind of revelation, a seeing, an illumination. In this way reason and the revelations of faith travel some ways together. You might even say that intellection is a type of revelation, a seeing of what is.

Master Theodore: How then do the truths of knowledge and the revelations of faith differ from one another?

Frederick II: This is a difficult question, Master Theodore, which I will attempt to answer in the following way. The truths of reason come to us in the first instance by a kind of seeing or illumination, what you might call a self-evidence which impresses itself upon us. From that are built up what we call demonstrations, which build upon these simple ideas by steps which are also self-evident. This is what we call logic, which I have studied with masters of logic for many years. In no other way can absolute knowledge be achieved.

Master Theodore: But in your book on hunting with falcons you build up knowledge in a different way.

Frederick II: Yes, but I begin with ideas as well. By naming what is and then connecting our ideas not by logical demonstration but as a guess or a hypothesis, I formulate a tentative conclusion. Then I test this conclusion against all cases that arise in the perceptible world. Here is where I improve upon the conclusions of Aristotle about birds. Much of what he wrote is not based upon first hand observation or testing but upon what I call hearsay, that is, the testimony of others. This testimony may or may not be reliable, and in Aristotle's case it often was not. By carefully observing what is, we can test our hypotheses and in this way achieve a rather high degree of certainty. This knowledge is not certain in the manner of deductions from simple ideas, and it must always be open to improvement. But in this manner we can achieve much useful knowledge which can guide us in the sensible world.

Master Theodore: How do the revelations of the monotheistic faiths differ? Are they not based in the first instance upon a kind of direct illumination as well?

Frederick II: Yes, but in a very different manner. The revelations of faith which are held by believers do not come directly to them; they are taught the revelations of others whom we call prophets. They do not arise from the immediate awareness of what is self-evident to believers. They must be taken on faith. It is not self-evident to a believer that god gave his commands to Moses on a tablet, or that Jesus is a part of god, or that allah will punish unbelievers in hell. Such things are not self-evident at all but depend upon the testimony of others. Maimonides rightly says without a belief in prophecy there is no belief in the Law.

Master Theodore: Do we not rely in many instances on the testimony of others? I may not have seen an act committed, but in a legal proceeding the testimony of others is sufficient.

Frederick II: It is always possible that others are not speaking the truth. I have frequently said that the stars do not lie, but my astrologers surely can.

Master Theodore: As we have discussed, religious faith requires trust in those who claim to have received direct revelations from god.

Frederick II: Yes, a prophet might have received what he believes is a direct revelation from god. There may be no doubt that he has come to believe certain things to be true based upon his experience. But what warrant has a prophet to assume his experience is from god? I may have a strong intimation that I should move my camp to a new city. By what right do I assume this is a message from god and not from my own mind which, having deliberated upon this question, has come to an inward conclusion?

Master Theodore: Do religious revelations differ in any other way from what you have called the inward workings of your mind?

Frederick II: Yes, in one important way. The followers of a faith believe in what they have heard, not what they have seen. Even the prophets of whom we have spoken have invariably heard messages from whom they suppose is god but have never seen god. As we have said, seeing is already a kind of intellection. Hearing is not. I have often said that "no certainty is attained by the ear." In this I have followed the ancient Greek philosophers. Heracleitus says, for example, "the eyes are more exact witnesses than the ears." The Pythagoreans spoke this way as well. And of course Plato chose to associate intellection with seeing rather than hearing. The Greek word *theoria* originally meant viewing, looking at or beholding.

Hearing is said to provide instruction regarding things which are unseen. It is not important for the Jews whether Moses has seen god or not, which he did not; what is important is what god spoke to him. This is surely true for Christians as well. The apostle Thomas was spoken ill of for not trusting what he had heard about Jesus, but demanded to see for himself. It is said that those who trust in the word of god without seeing are more to be praised. Paul speaks to this as well in Romans 10:17 where he says that "faith comes by hearing, and hearing by the word of God." And Muhammad never saw god but was told of god's commands by a messenger who spoke to him. And as this messenger was a spirit—the Qu'ran says that god "revealed a spirit" to Muhammad— one must suppose that Muhammad did not see this messenger either.

Master Theodore: The followers of these faiths must trust their messengers.

Frederick II: Yes, but as I have often said, no truth comes from hearsay. Through seeing comes knowledge and through hearing comes obedience. Why should the followers of faiths not follow what is revealed to them, rather than to a prophet who is long since dead?

Master Theodore: You are suggesting that reason is more democratic than the revelations of prophets.

Frederick II: Yes, reason is accessible to all. Adelard of Bath, who has translated many Arabic works into Latin, spoke well when he said to his nephew: "For I have acquired one type of learning, with reason as guide, from my Arabic teachers, while you, fettered by the appearance of authority, follow another, as a halter ... For your listeners do not understand that reason has been given to each person to distinguish between true and false, reason being the prime judge. If reason were not to be that universal judge, she would have been given to each one in vain." Why would god have given reason to all men if it were not to be used? Not all men will employ reason to the same degree, but what is true must be available in principle to all men.

Master Theodore: Reason can teach men much if they use it.

Frederick II: Yes, a great deal, though perhaps not all we might wish to know. If Aristotle is correct in saying that to know a thing truly is to know its cause, we will always find that full knowledge is beyond us. We can locate the causes of visible things in invisible forces, and we can know how they operate, but we seem never able to know these invisible forces directly or why they are as they are.

Master Theodore: The monotheistic faiths say that god is the invisible force—or will, as is more often said—behind all that occurs.

Frederick II: Yes, but as philosophers say, we do not come to know god directly but at best in a partial way. Who claims to know the essence of god? God is known, if at all, through his effects rather than through his essence.

Master Theodore: Is this not also true of any and all forces which act as causes?

Frederick II: This is just so. We speak of invisible forces which are the causes of what occurs, but these forces are not known directly by us. They too are known by their effects. Our reason makes an assumption that if motion occurs, there must be a cause of it. Indeed, as Maimonides says, philosophers assume nothing in the natural world is in vain and that all has a cause or a reason for being. We can speak about how these causes unfold but we do not for all of that know them directly. We may say that a certain plant causes sleepiness, and we can use that knowledge to good purpose. We might even be able to understand what it is about the plant which causes this effect. But as to the cause itself and why it is one way and not another, who is to say?

Master Theodore: Is this true then of all causes, including god or whatever secondary causes may exist?

Frederick II: Yes, we can know how they work, but not what they are in themselves. Aristotle says in the book we call his *Metaphysics* that "nature is the source of those things which contain in themselves as such a source of motion." In studying nature, we will learn how these causes operate, but we will not learn what they are in themselves. We can liken them to a push or a pull or an act of will, all of which we understand intuitively. But we will not know them directly.

Master Theodore: We may refer to them as *dunamis* or force or will or by any other word but we will not for that reason have direct knowledge of them.

Frederick II: We may express the operation of natural causes by mathematical formulas which explain how they work, just as the Pythagoreans thought would be possible. We may explain natural causes with simple formulas but we will not know why nature acts just as these formulas describe. If we say the area of a circle can be found by multiplying the radius times itself by the number 3.14 we will learn the area of any circle. But we do not know why this happens to be so. All we know is that it just is.

Master Theodore: We should study the operation of natural causes even if we do not know what they are or why they are as they are.

Frederick II: There is much to be learned in this manner. And it may turn out that some of these invisible forces operate in the same way in many different circumstances. This would be helpful to know. And I would say more. Studying these natural forces, even if they are invisible, is the only true way to gain—if only by inference—any knowledge of the first cause of things which many men call god. We simply cannot derive knowledge of why the world is as it is by contemplating the idea of god. Theologians can say that god must have made the world as he did, or that he might have made it differently. But how could this be known? Should we suppose there is knowledge of such a force as a god who might have made the world differently? Down this course lies only empty speculation.

To the contrary, it is by studying how the invisible forces in the world operate, that we are led to the idea of god in the first place. Reason has rightly been criticized for overreaching at times, as when it seeks to know why things happen rather than how they happen. But without reason we would never be led to the idea of god at all. This is why I favor Averroes so highly and al-Ghazali, for all his brilliance and passion, so little. If little or nothing at all can be known, how do we know of god and the creation? The entire world may or may not be contingent, but its operations are knowable. And the more we study it, the more we know of it.

Master Theodore: We do not so much gain knowledge of the world from inferences from a first cause, as we gain the idea of a first cause from knowledge of the world.

Frederick II: We cannot demonstrate that the first cause must have created the world just as it did or for what reason. We can say only that we have the world we have and that it somehow must have been caused to be as it is. When we strive to go beyond what reason can teach and say why the world must have come to be just the way it is, what does this speculation add to our experience of the world?

Master Theodore: Our knowing takes us to the idea of god.

Frederick II: There is no doubt there is an idea of god.

Master Theodore: Can you say then what these thoughts of yours mean for the future?

Frederick II: We know the "whatness" of things by our intellection of the ideas. But this does not by itself tell us much about the sensible world. There is no direct path from intellection of the ideas to knowledge of the sensible world. The ideas are tools which we must employ to gain that kind of knowledge.

Philosophers have often asked why what is, is. They might ask with equal justice why what occurs, occurs. And as Plato said, they will not find that the ideas cause motion in the sensible world to be just as it is. We men who are limited in what we can know should concern ourselves with how things work in the sensible world. This requires ideas, but the contemplation of ideas will never lead to knowledge of how things work in the sensible world, which is genuinely useful knowledge. Perhaps one day we will learn that the "what" of things will turn out to be the very same as the invisible forces of things. I am told that Plato hinted at this in his *Sophist*. He said there that being is the presence of a power to act or to be acted upon in even the slightest degree. In this way being and power are drawn together, suggesting that perhaps they are one and the same. But whether this is so or not, we will never learn until we study very carefully how invisible forces act in the world.

The Unconquerable Sun

Master Theodore: You seem to be saying two important things, one which has often been said before and one which is quite novel. You are saying that human reason has clear limitations. This has often been said before, especially by men of faith.

Frederick II: This is true. The ideas which we can know are known by us directly. But they are never the fullness of knowledge. They must be presupposed if there is to be such a thing as knowledge—which there is—but the ideas do not teach us more than that they are.

Master Theodore: The ideas, as we have said, allow us to see something of the "whatness" of what is.

Frederick II: Yes. We say, for example, there is an idea of justice. But this idea creates no justice in the world, nor does it tell us what is perfectly just in any circumstance. We might say too that there is an idea of mathematical equality. But this idea does not tell us what is and what is not equal in the sensible world. We might say there is an idea of god, but this does not tell us how he works, if he does, in the sensible world. We might make use of ideas when we say that one kind of falcon flies faster than another. But the idea of "faster" will tell us nothing about which falcons actually fly faster than others. Time would run out before all the examples we could offer. In each of these cases, and all others, our intellection of the ideas we employ will not tell us much about how the world in which we live works. The ideas will provide no certainty about these matters.

Master Theodore: This points to the novelty of your thinking. We cannot understand the way the world works, that is, its motions, by thinking only about ideas and their relationship to one another.

Frederick II: Yes, this is just so. Both Plato and the three monotheistic faiths have privileged what is at rest, because it is said to be unchanging or eternal and therefore more fully in being. Rest is understood as uniformity and motion, or at least certain types of it, as non-uniformity. But what if we doubt this? What if we say that some kinds of change are no less in being than what is changeless?

Master Theodore: Heracleitus seems to have said just this.

Frederick II: Yes, but his view as attributed by Aristotle, that it is not possible to step twice into the same river, is self-contradictory. For what changes must still abide in some way, or else how would we know it has changed? When he says we cannot step twice in the same river, it is still the same river into which we step. How else could he say this? Indeed, Heracleitus himself recognized this when he said in another passage that "In the same river, we both step and do not step."

What I am saying is very different. What if what changes does so with certain regularity and the regularity itself is unchanging? This would make certain kinds of change themselves changeless just as are certain kinds of rest. We would then no longer privilege rest over change, but consider both as equals.

Master Theodore: This would be a novel way of thinking.

Frederick II: Yes, but there are grounds for this in ancient Greek philosophy. For Plato has said that the Idea of the good—or the one, as many of his successors say—is not at rest or in motion, but is beyond both. Since both rest and motion exist, the Idea of the good or the one cannot be thought of as either rest or motion. Therefore the Idea of the Good is not eternally at rest, but is something beyond either rest or motion, beyond being and becoming. If we should determine that certain motions occur in unchanging ways how is such motion inferior to what is at rest? How is it less in being, as we might say? What moves is no more or less in need of explanation than what is at rest. What becomes in unchanging ways is no less important than what is at rest—because this becoming abides as surely as what is at rest. And it is no less appropriate to employ ideas to understand what is in regular motion than what is at rest.

Master Theodore: It has always been our tradition to assume that what moves requires a fuller explanation than what is at rest, which seems to require no explanation.

Frederick II: Yes, but motion is no less natural than rest and no more or less in need of explanation than what is at rest. What thinkers have done is to acknowledge that what is beyond being is neither at rest nor in motion— and then promptly forget this, thinking instead of being as what is at rest. It is every bit as worthy to study the invisible and unchanging causes of becoming as those of being, since to speak properly, neither partakes more truly of being than the other.

Master Theodore: Aristotle aims to understand the world of becoming.

Frederick II: Yes. He does not doubt the existence of ideas, but he knows they do not explain anything in the sensible world. He understands ideas not as a way to gain direct knowledge of the sensible world, but as tools to be used in that process. But he goes wrong in asserting that the sublunar world moves in a different way than the rest of the cosmos. The entire cosmos is moved in the same way throughout. Here the Christian Philoponus, who criticizes Aristotle on the eternity of the cosmos, is closer to the truth. Even the thoughtful Maimonides wrongly follows Aristotle in thinking that the sublunar world is governed by different principles than the remainder of the cosmos.

Master Theodore: Rest is not to be privileged over motion.

Frederick II: They are both to be understood. But Aristotle shares Plato's view that only what is the result of reasoned intention can be orderly and knowable, and that nature remains in part always beyond what is reasonable. It is, in Plato's words, a kind of necessity which bounds the power of reason to order the world. What I am saying is very different: there is as much order to be found in the sensible world as in the products of reasoned intention. This is because nature operates according to orderly causes which we can learn by studying them.

Master Theodore: So we are not to assume that nature is a vast disorderly sphere of chance, in which all things have their own unique power of self-motion? Rather, that nature operates according to patterns or laws which we can discover?

Frederick II: Just so. What is meant by "necessity" must be understood in a very different manner from that of the ancient Greek philosophers. It is not that which stands as a bound to the intentions of a rational creator, but is the unfailing regularity with which the sensible world operates. We might adopt the language of some recent theologians, who speak of laws of nature. And if we ask the proper questions of nature, we may then discover these natural laws and use them to our advantage.

Master Theodore: Physics then would consist of a search for what is in nature similar to what theologians call natural laws.

Frederick II: Just so.

Master Theodore: It has always been thought until now that the many and various causes which move different parts of nature exist as a kind of occult power within each of these diverse parts of nature.

Frederick II: Yes, consider the case of plants. It has been said, and correctly so, that certain plants have the power to induce sleepiness and others have the power to aid digestion, and so forth. We seem to have as many occult powers as there are effects. But it seems likely that we shall discover that the causes of nature are fewer in number and more general in scope. Powers which now seem to inhere uniquely within each part of nature will turn out to be more general in kind and broader in scope. This will allow us to discover many different ways to achieve the same ends.

Master Theodore: Is this somehow to say, as do the Asharites, that god is the one and sole cause of all that occurs, no matter how different these occurrences may be?

Frederick II: Not at all. We can say that god causes all that occurs, but this is to say both very much and very little at the same time. One may say this, but then one must do the difficult work of studying how nature actually works in order to understand the regular and unchanging causes of its motions.

Master Theodore: Simply to attribute all that occurs to one cause is to learn very little.

Frederick II: Yes. And this mistake is made by ancient philosophers in a different way. They assert that the *end* of all things, that is, what they desire, is the good. How could we know this, and further, how would it help us to understand the world? A "nature" is that which uniformly behaves in the same way, not that which has the same ends as another entity of its class. Many things which move seem to have no end at all, and to suppose they do is simply to impute to all of nature the human quality of desire. The world itself, and everything within it, cannot properly be said to have any end or purpose at all.

Master Theodore: The regularity of what becomes is no more or less real than the regularity of what abides?

Frederick II: Ideas are eternal and thus changeless. But the manner in which we employ the Ideas should be the same to study what becomes as what is at rest.

Master Theodore: And it would be fair to say that our reason is limited in both cases, to what we can know of the changing as well as the changeless.

Frederick II: Yes, we might understand how the invisible forces of nature operate, but we will have no more or less intuition about what they are or why they are. This seems to be a limit of reason, that we can know very little of the invisible forces in their essential nature. This has always been the problem up against which all negative theologies founder. And it will be no less the case for those invisible forces which seem to move the sensible world. They are a placeholder for what we do not know of causes in their essence, much less why they occur just as they do.

Master Theodore: You are describing a world which seems to have no overarching end or purpose. This is a world which is, and apparently always will be, somewhat mysterious and unable to be known through the language of human intentions.

Frederick II: Yes, this is where these thoughts lead us. Men cannot disprove there is a first cause of motion, which might be called god, but they will instead busy themselves with coming to know how motion and change occur in the sensible world.

Master Theodore: God's role will not be disproven, but his presence will recede as more is learned about the unchanging secondary causes that operate in the world.

Frederick II: Just so, Master Theodore.

Master Theodore: Does this mean that contemplation of first causes will disappear as a human activity?

Frederick II: By no means. Men will continue to speculate about first causes and how and why the world exists as it does. This is a deeply pleasurable activity, one to which thoughtful men are drawn irresistibly like iron filings to a magnet. But men will find less connection between these speculations and knowledge of how and in what ways invisible forces operate in the world. One might reasonably guess that the speculations of what since Aristotle we have called metaphysics will never disappear. But they will lose their connection to the sciences which understand how the natural world operates.

Master Theodore: What else shall we conclude from this?

Frederick II: In such a world philosophers will appear less dangerous. The claims of whether the world is eternal or created, for example, will not affect the search for knowledge about how the sensible world operates. This is very different from today, where such views shape how men think about the world. There will perhaps be fewer charges of heresy than we see today. If I might offer an example, I cannot learn anything at all about how to train falcons by pretending to knowledge of whether the world is eternal or created.

Master Theodore: Are there other consequences?

Frederick II: Yes, it will be more widely assumed that it is a mistake to worship ideas. As Plato makes clear, ideas do not create anything. They have in this way their uses but no power.

Master Theodore: Does this include the idea of god?

Frederick II: Yes. The ideas, including the idea of god, do not create anything. They are tools we use to understand what is. There is no purpose to worship these, as if they were powerful and demand our obedience. Both those who worship the idea of god and those who worship what they wrongly suppose is their own ability to create ideas are equally misled. Ideas help us to know what is, but they do not create what is.

Master Theodore: We might think of ideas as the pre-condition for knowing what is, rather than for creating what is.

Frederick II: That is well said, Master Theodore. The monotheistic faiths and Plato's *Timaeus* are alike in this regard. They go behind the sensible world, so to say, to find an invisible force which created the world. It is agreed by the wisest men of all faiths, and by Plato as well, that this force is not tangible but is an intangible spirit which exists nowhere and everywhere. This force may be described for common men as possessing tangible qualities like a body, eyes to see, ears to hear, and human emotions, but wise men know this cannot be so.

Master Theodore: Is it not the invisible powers that men worship?

Frederick II: Yes, but the ideas of such powers are but pale reflections of the powers themselves. Our idea of god, for example, is said to be inadequate to whatever god exists.

Master Theodore: When men worship god they actually worship an idea of the invisible force of god?

Frederick II: Yes, just so.

Master Theodore: Is this true of our other ideas as well?

Frederick II: Consider that mysterious entity which we call time. Time is not an entity or a substance to be found in the perceptible world. Time is an idea which we use to measure. Time is an idea which we can know through intellection. But we must cut time into pieces, as it were, if we are to make use of this idea. The same is also true of the idea of space or emptiness—what Plato calls a receptacle—which becomes useful only when it is cut into pieces in such ways that we call dimensions.

Master Theodore: Your thinking points away from worshipping ideas, whether of that which is perceptible or that which is invisible.

Frederick II: Yes, and at the very center of our thinking stands the sun, which is the most important of all that is perceptible. When we go behind the sun, as it were, to worship the idea of a force which has created the sun, what have we really added to our knowledge?

Master Theodore: Were early philosophers correct then to worship the sun?

Frederick II: I do not say this. The three monotheistic faiths say it is a grave error to worship the sun, and in this they are correct—but not for the reason they think. Many ancient civilizations worshipped the sun. If one wishes to portray them as thoughtless or silly to do this, one would say they were worshipping the fiery ball in the sky. This would suggest that men had chosen the sun from a number of possible perceptible objects including the sun, the moon, the stars or even earthly objects such as a golden calf. It is to suppose they do so because the object itself is to be venerated.

Master Theodore: This would misjudge those people who reverence the sun.

Frederick II: Very much so. Such people are not worshipping the fiery ball in the sky, but its power to make possible, or to enable, all that is and all that occurs on earth, perhaps even the existence of the earth itself. They offer thanks to what enables our world and our lives to be at all. This is neither crazy nor mistaken. Maimonides speaks honestly when he says that idols or "zelem" are not worshipped because of their form but because of what they symbolize.

Master Theodore: The perceptible sun is a kind of symbol.

Frederick II: Yes, as it has always been. Macrobius makes clear in his interesting book *Saturnalia* that the gods which the great preponderance of the ancients worshipped—the Egyptians, the Assyrians, the Greeks and the Romans—were all associated in one way or another with the sun. The three monotheistic faiths have judged correctly from their standpoint that worship of the sun is the idolatry *par excellence.*

Master Theodore: The sun is the most natural perceptible object toward which to display reverence.

Frederick II: Yes, but again it is not the fiery ball as a perceptible object, but the power of the sun which enables all that occurs in the perceptible world. In my early youth I was instructed by the teacher the pope assigned to educate me that reverence for the sun was not proper, that reverence for Jesus was proper. I recall wondering at my young age why it made more sense to revere a Jewish carpenter, wonderful as he was, than the sun itself. One might say the same about a wanderer in the desert of Sinai or a man in the hills of Arabia.

Master Theodore: But it can be said that the sun is not the only pre-condition of our existence.

Frederick II: This is surely true. There are perhaps many. I could point to my parents, for example. Though I did not know my father, I owe a deep and unpayable debt to my parents Henry VI and Constance for my existence in just the way I am. An attitude of appreciation, even reverence, is appropriate toward them as well. This reverence may not require a special rite, such as the requirement to bow five times in their direction each day, but rather an attitude of thanks.

Master Theodore: In many cases it seems the rites of the monotheistic faiths, which are meant as a means to express reverence, become the ends themselves.

Frederick II: This is quite true. The rites of faith are properly understood as a path to take believers to a reverence for their god, not as objects of dispute and contention themselves.

Master Theodore: Among the many pre-conditions of life on earth the sun would seem to have a very high standing.

Frederick II: Yes. No wise man thinks the sun alone enables our life to be. No wise man thinks the sun can tell us how we should live our lives or that reverence for the sun can compel the sun to change our fate. Praying to the sun to advance our own ends in life makes no sense. What there is to be grateful for is not the sun's power to respond to our prayers, but its role in enabling our lives to be at all. Wise men have never thought the sun, the moon, the planets or the stars are gods in themselves, but as underlying forces which seem quite necessary for our existence.

Master Theodore: Let us return to how ideas and the sun stand in relation to one another.

Frederick II: With ideas we are able to know the sun as the sun. We are able to name the sun and to seek after its miraculous power. But we should not say that an idea has created the sun, because it has not. And there is one more point to make which is no less important.

Master Theodore: Please explain.

Frederick II: Ideas are tools which enable us not only to know the sun as sun. This is true for all objects that exist. But in the case of the sun there is one power which we do not find in other objects in the perceptible world, at least not to the same extent. That is to provide us the gift of light.

Master Theodore: Light is provided to us not by an idea but by the sun.

Jeff Bergner

Frederick II: Yes, Plato is correct when he says the Ideas, and especially the Idea of the good, are to be understood by an analogy to the sun. But it is proper to say the Idea of the good is modeled after the sun rather than the sun after the Idea of the good. Without the light of the sun we would have no ability to see either what is in the perceptible world or the ideas of what is in the perceptible world.

Master Theodore: We come back in a way to where we began our discussion. Light is most important.

Frederick II: Just so. Whoever wrote that light is the first principle of all was very wise. Without light we cannot exist; but without light we cannot know ideas, nor can we therefore achieve any knowledge at all.

Master Theodore: Is the sun or is the light what is important?

Frederick II: The sun that we exist and the light that we know. I would far prefer an attitude of reverence for light and for that which provides light—the sun—than for an idea which provides no light at all.

Master Theodore: Do you believe that because the sun provides light, the sun must be greater than the light which it causes?

Frederick II: Ancient philosophers always said that what creates is greater than what is created. Why did they think so? They supposed that what creates might create differently. A sculptor might have chosen to fashion a different sculpture, or none at all. What creates therefore has more power, and is therefore said to be more in being than what is created. But this relies upon the thought that the creator is free to do otherwise than he has done. If the creator, however, has no choice but to create in just the way he does, for what reason should we look at the creator as greater than what he has created? Dionysius, who is sometimes known as the Areopagite, says the sun has no choice but to give light to all. The sun has no choice, it would seem, but to provide light. This is its nature to do so. I make no judgment as to whether the sun or light is greater; it is enough that they are. Why should we not be thankful that such a nature as the sun exists?

Master Theodore: What there is should be looked at with reverence then?

Frederick II: Yes, it is wrong to depreciate the world we have as an

181

imperfect imitation of anything. We should not have contempt for the world which we have by seeing it as a poor imitation of an idea, be it the Ideas of Plato or the gods of the monotheistic faiths. For better to assume the attitude of David of Dinant, who sees the world as the perceptible image of god, not an imperfect imitation of god.

Master Theodore: It seems the three monotheistic faiths each recognize the importance of light, even though they believe it is a creation of an idea or spirit.

Frederick II: In the book of Revelation Jesus says he is "the root and the offspring of David, the morning star." The morning star of course is Venus which was called Lucifer or the "light bringer," a title which has strangely been associated in recent times with Satan.

Let me conclude our discussion in this way. Almost every faith, including the three monotheistic faiths, speaks favorably of light; they associate their god with light. Let me speak specifically of our Christian faith here in the west. In the gospel of John Jesus says "I am the light of the world." Christians look to Jesus as this light. This is usually understood to mean that following Jesus is the way to light up the world for us.

But consider this in another way, emphasizing the word "is." It is then said that "Christ *is* the light of the world." The divinity is the light and the light is the divinity. Light is not only a gift, but is *the* gift. We might say that light not only reveals, but that it is the revelation itself. Orthodox Christian writers like Albert reject David of Dinant's view that the world is the perceptible image of god. They say that Jesus is the perceptible image of god. Perhaps these two ideas are not in the end so very different in what they aim to teach. Light is a gift each and every day, for which we should always be grateful. An attitude of reverence toward the sun is a decent way to express this.

www.ingramcontent.com/pod-product-compliance
Lightning Source LLC
Chambersburg PA
CBHW032058080426
42733CB00006B/333